The LMS Princess Coronation Pacifics
The Final Years & Preservation

Front cover photo:
46245 *City of London* at Willesden shed in early 1964 after the closure of Camden shed the previous year. (MLS Collection)

Back cover photos:
46242 *City of Glasgow* at Carlisle Kingmoor depot, 16 June 1963. (A.C. Gilbert/MLS Collection)

The preserved and re-streamlined 6229 *Duchess of Hamilton* at the National Railway Museum, York, 10 December 2021. (David Maidment)

The LMS Princess Coronation Pacifics
The Final Years & Preservation

DAVID MAIDMENT

AN IMPRINT OF PEN & SWORD BOOKS LTD.
YORKSHIRE – PHILADELPHIA

First published in Great Britain in 2023 by
Pen & Sword Transport
An imprint of Pen & Sword Books Ltd
Yorkshire - Philadelphia

Copyright © David Maidment, 2023

ISBN 978 1 39902 262 0

The right of David Maidment to be identified as author of this work has been asserted by him in accordance with the Copyright, Designs and Patents Act 1988.

A CIP catalogue record for this book is available from the British Library.

All rights reserved. No part of this book may be reproduced or transmitted in any form or by any means, electronic or mechanical including photocopying, recording or by any information storage and retrieval system, without permission from the Publisher in writing.

Typeset in Palatino by SJmagic DESIGN SERVICES, India.
Printed and bound in India by Replika Press Pvt. Ltd.

Pen & Sword Books Ltd incorporates the Imprints of Pen & Sword Books Archaeology, Atlas, Aviation, Battleground, Discovery, Family History, History, Maritime, Military, Naval, Politics, Railways, Select, Transport, True Crime, Fiction, Frontline Books, Leo Cooper, Praetorian Press, Seaforth Publishing, Wharncliffe and White Owl.

For a complete list of Pen & Sword titles please contact:

PEN & SWORD BOOKS LIMITED
George House, Units 12 & 13, Beevor Street, Off Pontefract Road,
Barnsley, South Yorkshire, S71 1HN, England
E-mail: enquiries@pen-and-sword.co.uk
Website: www.pen-and-sword.co.uk

Or

PEN AND SWORD BOOKS
1950 Lawrence Rd, Havertown, PA 19083, USA
E-mail: Uspen-and-sword@casematepublishers.com
Website: www.penandswordbooks.com

All royalties from this book will be donated to the Railway Children charity [reg. no. 1058991] [www.railwaychildren.org.uk]

Other books by David Maidment:
Novels (Religious historical fiction)
The Child Madonna, Melrose Books, 2009
The Missing Madonna, PublishNation, 2012
The Madonna and her Sons, PublishNation, 2015
The Reluctant Traitor, PublishNation, 2021

Novels (Railway fiction)
Lives on the Line, Max Books, 2013
Steamy Stories, PublishNation, 2021 (Short stories)

Non-fiction (Railways)
The Toss of a Coin, PublishNation, 2014
A Privileged Journey, Pen & Sword, 2015
An Indian Summer of Steam, Pen & Sword, 2015
Great Western Eight-Coupled Heavy Freight Locomotives, Pen & Sword, 2015
Great Western Moguls and Prairies, Pen & Sword, 2016
Southern Urie and Maunsell 2-cylinder 4-6-0s, Pen & Sword, 2016
Great Western Small-Wheeled Double-Framed 4-4-0s, Pen & Sword, 2017
The Development of the German Pacific Locomotive, Pen & Sword, 2017
Great Western Large-Wheeled Double-Framed 4-4-0s, Pen & Sword, 2017
Great Western Counties, 4-4-0s, 4-4-2Ts & 4-6-0s, Pen & Sword, 2018
Southern Maunsell Moguls and Tank Engines, Pen & Sword, 2018
Southern Maunsell 4-4-0s, Pen & Sword, 2019
Great Western Granges, Pen & Sword, 2019
Cambrian Railways Gallery, Pen & Sword, 2019
Great Western Panniers, Pen & Sword, 2019
Great Western Kings, Pen & Sword, 2020
Great Western & Absorbed Railway 0-6-2Ts, Pen & Sword, 2020
Drummond's L&SWR Passenger & Mixed Traffic Locomotives, Pen & Sword, 2020
Southern 0-6-0 Tender Locomotives, Pen & Sword, 2021
LNER 4-6-0 Locomotives, Pen & Sword, 2021
Midland & LMS 4-4-0s, Pen & Sword, 2021
Great Western Castle 4-6-0 Locomotives, 1923-1959, Pen & Sword, 2022
Great Western Castle 4-6-0 Locomotives, The Final Years 1960-1965, Pen & Sword, 2022
Great Western Castle 4-6-0 Locomotives, In the Preservation Era, Pen & Sword, 2023
Four-coupled Tank Locomotives, Built by the Great Western Railway, Pen & Sword, 2023
Four-coupled Tank Locomotives, Absorbed by the Great Western Railway, Pen & Sword, 2023
The Princess Coronation Pacific Locomotives, 1937-1956, Pen & Sword, 2023

Non-fiction (Street Children)
The Other Railway Children, PublishNation, 2012
Nobody ever listened to me, PublishNation, 2012

CONTENTS

	Acknowledgements	6
	Introduction	7
Chapter 1	Recap	9
Chapter 2	1957–60	12
Chapter 3	The Final Years, 1960–1964	39
Chapter 4	Personal Experience	77
Chapter 5	Railwaymen remember	92
Chapter 6	Preservation	112
Chapter 7	Conclusions	128
	Colour Section	137
	Appendix	169
	Bibliography	176
	Index	177

ACKNOWLEDGEMENTS

I continue to pay a debt of gratitude to the authors of those many books listed in the bibliography who have endeavoured over the years to build a comprehensive picture and history of the Princess Coronation pacifics – the 'Duchesses'. I have used their books as research as well as drawing on my own personal experiences. I am grateful and privileged to have enjoyed conversations with, and received precious material from, former Crewe drivers (and firemen in the time of Duchesses on Crewe's most challenging turns), Les Jackson, Neil Cadman and Bill Andrew and also Crewe Works fitter, Keith Collier, and am indebted to Crewe Heritage Centre Hon Chairman Gordon Heddon for setting these opportunities up. I thank Bob Meanley, the co-author of one of the definitive books on the class, for undertaking to review this manuscript and drawing my attention to errors and omissions and enabling me to correct them and providing the description and photographs of the re-streamlining of 6229.

I am particularly grateful once again to members of the Manchester Locomotive Society and in particular Paul Shackcloth, who has given me access to the vast collection of 'Duchess' photographs and slides in the archives of the clubroom on Stockport station and permission to publish them free of any fee as I am, as usual, donating all the royalties from the book to the Railway Children charity (www.railwaychildren.org.uk) which I founded in 1995 to support street and runaway children on the railway and bus stations of the world as well as on our own UK railway stations. Many of the photographs do not bear the name of the photographer or copyright holder and whilst I have tried to contact those where possible I ask for forgiveness if I have missed any. If you are one of those, please contact the publisher and I will try to make amends.

I thank my editor Carol Trow and my Pen & Sword Production Manager, Janet Brookes, Commissioning Editor John Scott-Morgan and the whole Pen & Sword team for their professional work in producing once more a book of which I and they can feel proud, despite the pressure of ever increasing costs.

INTRODUCTION

In January 1957 I commenced temporary work at Old Oak Common to fill the gap between leaving school in December and starting my German language and literature course at University College, London, in September. One of the immediate benefits, apart from living and breathing alongside GW Kings and Castles, was to earn the right, after a month, to use quarter rate privilege railway tickets and my evenings began to be filled with explorations around other London termini searching where I could travel out and back at a reasonable hour. In addition to sorties to Swindon, Oxford and Banbury, I was soon adding Rugby and Peterborough to my itineraries – on Saturdays stretching to Crewe and Doncaster as well as sampling the Summer Saturday meanderings of engines from my home shed.

After joining British Railways permanently in August 1960, my evening and weekend jaunts expanded to include the lengths of the East and West Coast main lines, though by this time I was having to search diligently for steam amid the growing number of English Electric Type 4s (class 40) on both routes. I thus saw the twilight years of the Stanier pacifics, the *Lakes Express* providing the last certainty of finding a Duchess on express duty. As this book is covering those final years, I am able to share my personal experiences, the surprises and the disappointments, in Chapter 4.

I hope that most of you will have already purchased and enjoyed my first volume, but in case some of you have come straight to this era as it has more particular memories of your own, I am including a short 'recap' chapter to highlight the main developments which led to thirty-seven capable pacifics available for the main West Coast heavy traffic at the start of 1957. You might well argue – certainly compared to the number of pacifics on the East Coast route – that this was not enough, even including the dozen earlier 'Princess Royals'.

Other books have been written concentrating in particular on two of the Duchesses that have been preserved, but I have not only included much material about 6229 and 6233 but have the words of Les Jackson and Bill Andrew who drove these locomotives in the preservation era, and with Neil Cadman, remember their nights on the Perth run, firing Crewe North's Duchess turns. And a Crewe Works fitter, Keith Collier, remembers them during their overhauls in the Works and on the road and holds somewhat controversial views of their performance in comparison with that of Stanier's earlier pacifics (and 'Royal Scots').

I have therefore tried to bring together in these two books a comprehensive history of this superb class of locomotives – a general technical description, history of construction and appearance, operation and performance, brought up to date with the current situation of the three preserved engines and adding my own personal experience and that of firemen, drivers and works fitter of the engines, as well as finding a fresh source of many unpublished photographs in the archives of the Manchester Locomotive Society. I have treasured models of the class on my own 'OO' gauge layout – Hornby models that I repainted in BR green and renumbered 46232 and 46250 after engines of which I had personal memories, similarly 46244 that was purchased after being 'crownlined' and finished in the 1958 red livery and most recently the new Hornby model of 46257. I also own a display model of the streamlined 6225 that was presented to me after I was the speaker a few years ago at the annual Crewe Dinner held in London – a reunion of past Crewe Engineering Graduates and their guests – I was substituting at the last moment for the planned speaker, Boris Johnson, who not unsurprisingly found he had another more pressing engagement!

I offer this book therefore to those interested in general railway history, to modellers and those just enthused by what even a GWR enthusiast has to admit was one of the very best of steam locomotives that graced the metals of the United Kingdom.

David Maidment,
September 2023

Chapter 1
RECAP

William Stanier came to the London Midland & Scottish Railway (LMSR) in 1932 after a turbulent and controversial period in the early years of the company. Henry Fowler was meeting resistance from the traffic department and the former Midland Railway management hierarchy who – with that company's policy of running frequent lightly loaded expresses – poured doubt on Fowler's attempt to equip the company with larger pacific locomotives of either simple or compound expansion. Crewe Works was still building 4P compound 4-4-0s for main line express traction at a time when the LNER were using Gresley A1 (later A3) pacifics, the Great Western had more than seventy Kings and Castles and were building more, and Maunsell was equipping the Southern with the 'Scotch' King Arthurs and the 'Lord Nelsons'. Realising the unsuitability of the Compounds for the heavy West Coast services – and the amount of costly double-heading – a hurried order for the three-cylinder 'Royal Scots' was placed with the North British company, with more subsequently built at Derby.

One of Stanier's first decisions was to stop the construction of the Compounds – Crewe was halfway through a programme building ten (935-944) with more planned, and all after 939 were cancelled. Within a year, 6200 *The Princess Royal* and 6201 *Princess Elizabeth* were being tested and entering service, followed in 1934 by the experimental Turbomotive 6202 and the production run of 6203-6212 by 1935. A further order for 6213-6217 was intended but Stanier had second thoughts and encouraged his Chief Draftsman, Tom Coleman, to redesign the pacific with the biggest boiler that the loading gauge could take. Coleman did the detailed work, modified the motion design and got it approved by Stanier, who bowed to the wishes of the LMS Board constructing the first ten, renumbered 6220-6229, as streamliners to capture the public's imagination and match the developments of Gresley on the LNER. These engines took the railway world by storm in 1937 with the introduction of the *Coronation Scot* and the inaugural record breaking (and nearly catastrophic) trip when 114mph was claimed on the descent from Whitmore Bank into Crewe. Non-streamlined 6230-6234 followed in 1938 (thought to be much preferred by Stanier himself) and in 1939 on test 6234 *Duchess of Abercorn* produced a power output unsurpassed in British steam traction experience.

More streamliners followed but the onset of the Second World War in September 1939 brought an end to the high speed running. The construction of 6235-6244 continued as their power was valued for troop trains and restricted but heavily loaded passenger services. More were built during the war – 6245-6248 still in streamlined form, then 6249-6252 in conventional form and 6253-6255 near the end of the war. Stanier's successor, Henry Ivatt, updated the design slightly and 6256 and 6257 followed in 1947 and 1948, to be tested and assessed against the prototype LMS main line diesels, 10000 and 10001.

At the end of the war, a programme of de-streamlining took place as high speed running in its aftermath was not considered and improved access for maintenance was the priority. The de-streamlined pacifics were known by the spotters as 'semis' because of the shape of the smokebox which had fitted under the streamlining and was initially retained. In 1948 46236 *City of Bradford* took part in the

10 • THE LMS PRINCESS CORONATION PACIFICS, THE FINAL YEARS & PRESERVATION

46228 *Duchess of Rutland* outshopped from Crewe Works in 1958 in lined crimson livery, 29 June 1958. (MLS Collection)

One of Camden's star Duchesses in 1957/8 was 46245 *City of London*, seen here at Crewe North depot in 1958.

locomotive exchanges and ran on test to Leeds via the East Coast, Plymouth via the 'Berks & Hants' and Waterloo-Exeter. The tests were indecisive as the locomotives were not driven in a consistent way, some of the men – including the driver of 46236 – seeing the minimum fuel use as a priority, so 46236 hardly demonstrated what it was capable of.

The Stanier pacifics were subject to a number of livery changes in the early years of nationalisation, settling on the dark green similar to the former GWR livery, after a short-lived appearance in Caledonian blue. This was then the standard livery for the whole class until 1957 when a few selected engines (never the Scottish based pacifics) emerged from Crewe in maroon.

Services were accelerated in the mid-1950s, and the Duchesses began to show what they were capable of on trains like the *Royal Scot* and *Midday Scot* as well as on the heavy Merseyside expresses. Some of their work – especially that of the Crewe based engines – was on the heavy night sleeper services that regularly loaded to 500 tons or more, requiring sterling performance on Grayrigg, Shap and Beattock banks – though rarely recorded.

The lion & wheel emblem was replaced by the heraldic device from around 1957 and in December 1957 a decision was made to repaint some of the 'Princess Royals' and 'Coronations' in the LMS maroon livery. Sixteen were chosen (and four of the earlier pacifics). Only the LMR based engines were repainted thus as it was the LM Board that authorised the policy. I have seen a suggestion that the engines used mainly for the night sleeper work remained green as they would not be seen by the public but this seems unlikely. The suggestion was made by a Crewe based engineman and it may be that one of the foremen there allocated green engines to the overnight Perth sleepers for that reason and used its red engines on the London and Scottish day trains.

The engines painted maroon were: 46225/26/28/29/36/38/40/43-48/51/54/56. Some were lined LMS style and some BR style. Nameplates were black with polished letters and surrounds. Full details and dates of all livery changes are in the appendix, pages 171 and 172.

The Harrow & Wealdstone crash survivor, 46242 *City of Glasgow,* in BR standard green and later tender emblem, at Carlisle Kingmoor depot, 16 June 1963. (MLS Collection)

Crewe North's 46228 *Duchess of Rutland* in BR maroon, at Polmadie depot, Glasgow, c1960. Polmadie's standard 4MT tank 80007 is alongside. (Photomatic/MLS Collection)

Chapter 2
1957–60

The June LMR timetable for 1957 had nineteen mile-a-minute booked schedules on the West Coast main line, the fastest being the 7.55am Euston-Liverpool between Watford Junction and Crewe (62.4 mph) and the longest being the new *Caledonian* between Euston and Carlisle each way at 61.7 mph. Some 2,512 miles were booked at this speed, approximately half being Duchess hauled, the rest being on the Euston-Birmingham route. The Midland main line had a further 1,266 miles, while the Western Region could boast twenty-four trains at this speed over 2,294 miles. The Eastern Region barely reached 1,000 miles and the Southern had just one – the Down *Atlantic Coast Express* to Salisbury. Electrification work on the West Coast main line commenced in 1957 and the Crewe-Manchester section was opened to electric traction in 1959. One of the first 1957 runs on the 7.55 Euston with a near 500 ton load demonstrated that time could be kept even with the inclusion of two permanent way slacks and two severe signal checks. Arrival at Watford was 1½ minutes early but departure was 2 minutes late.

Watford Junction-Crewe,

46244 *King George VI* – Camden

15 chs, 448/485 tons

Edge Hill crew

7.55am Euston – Liverpool/Manchester

Miles	Location	Times	Speeds		Gradients
0	Watford Junction	00.00		2 L	
10.6	Berkhamsted	-	62 / pws 20*		1/335 R
14.3	Tring	20.06	55	6 L	1/335 R
18.7	Cheddington	-	85		1/333 F
22.8	Leighton Buzzard	-	80		
29.3	Bletchley	31.49	74	5¾ L	L
35	Wolverton	-	84		
42.5	Roade	42.04	68	5 L	1/330 R
45.4	Blisworth	44.28	80	4½ L	1/320 F
52.3	Weedon	51.35	pws 30*/72	5½ L	
57.9	Welton	-	73		1/350 R
65.2	Rugby	62.42	40*	4¾ L	
79.7	Nuneaton	76.19	83	4¼ L	1/320 F

Watford Junction-Crewe,

46244 *King George VI* – Camden

15 chs, 448/485 tons

Edge Hill crew

7.55am Euston – Liverpool/Manchester

Miles	Location	Times	Speeds		Gradients
89.1	Polesworth	-	74		1/321 F
92.6	Tamworth	86.07	85/83	1 L	L
98.9	Lichfield	90.40	86/72	¾ E	1/331 R
106.9	Rugeley	96.59	79	1 E	
	Colwich	-	sig stops		
116.2	Stafford	111.24	49*	3½ L	
130.3	Whitmore	124.08	72/68		1/398 R
135.9	Betley Road	128.39	86		1/177 F
	Basford Hall	-	sig stand		
140.7	Crewe	136.34	(121 net)	2½ L	

A couple of years later, substantial decelerations took place in schedules south of Crewe to provide recovery time to take the electrification engineering delays and diversions into account. When the electrification work was minimal and the road was clear, some trains in the early 1960s could disconcert people coming to greet passengers by arriving up to 45 minutes early! On the other hand, before the major work affected schedules too much, there was a flowering of performance from the summer timetable of 1957 with the *Royal Scot* on a 7¼ hour schedule and introduction of the *Caledonian* in both directions with a light load (280 ton limit), 8.30am from Glasgow returning in the late afternoon in 6 hours 40 minutes, almost restoring the 6½ hour schedules of the pre-war *Coronation Scot* with the one stop only at Carlisle. Two Camden engines worked the inaugural trains – 46242 on the Down and 46229 on the Up. For the summer timetable in 1958 only, a second *Caledonian* was experimentally introduced with a 7.45am departure from Euston and a late afternoon return to the capital. The 1957 and 1958 *Caledonians* were diagrammed for a Camden Duchess, returning on the next morning's 8.30am Glasgow, whilst the second 1958 train was a Polmadie Duchess in both directions. The extra 1958 service stopped additionally at Crewe northbound and Stafford southbound to give connections to the Birmingham area. The train was regularly diesel hauled from 1962.

Apart from the *Caledonian* and the night Crewe-Perth turns, a decision was made to change engines at Crewe and Carlisle on the day Scottish expresses so the allocation of Duchesses to Crewe in particular was boosted, although the *Royal Scot* engine still worked through to Glasgow on the theoretically non-stop Saturday service in the summer. The allocation of the Duchesses in 1957 was:

Camden: 46229, 46236, 46237, 46239-46242, 46244, 46245, 46247, 46250, 46253, 46254, 46256, 46257 (15)

Crewe: 46225, 46228, 46233-46235, 46243, 46246, 46248, 46249, 46251, 46252 (11)

Carlisle
Upperby: 46226, 46238, 46255
Polmadie: 46220-46224, 46227, 46230-46232 (9)

In the later 1950s, the number of enthusiasts timing trains and sending their experiences to Cecil J. Allen and O.S. Nock for publication in the *Railway Magazine* and *Trains Illustrated* increased significantly, especially after the announcement of impending traction changes in the 1955 Railway Modernisation Plan. It was realised that main line steam train haulage would soon diminish and there were efforts to record performance before the chance was lost. The Duchesses also hauled a number of other named expresses at this time including *The Red Rose, The Manxman, The Shamrock, The Empress Voyageur, The Irish Mail, The Emerald Isle Express, The Ulster Express* and *The Lakes Express*. North of the border they could be seen occasionally on *The Waverley* to Edinburgh and *The Thames-Clyde Express* to Glasgow via the G&SWR route, both taking over from Midland Division engines from Leeds Holbeck that had worked to Carlisle via Settle. However, train timing enthusiasts seem to have restricted themselves to the main Euston – Glasgow route, or both Cecil J. Allen and O.S. Nock in their regular magazine columns confined their writings to the *Caledonian, Royal Scot* and *Midday Scot* where the greatest effort seems to have been recorded.

The newly accelerated *Royal Scot* and *Caledonian* services in particular attracted many train recorders. 46221 *Queen Elizabeth* on the *Royal Scot* with 8 coaches, 261/280 tons, passed Lancaster at 76mph, touched 80 at Hest Bank, 83 at Carnforth, 77 minimum of the 1 in 134 to the summit before Burton & Holme, a full 88 at Milnthorpe and then a 20mph p-way check on the 1 in 104 of Grayrigg Bank from which 46221 astonishingly recovered to 52mph before the summit. 83mph before Tebay was too much for the train in front and 46221 and its train were brought to a stand at Scout Green Box right in the middle of the 1 in 75 to Shap summit. After a half minute stand, 46221 got away cleanly and topped Shap at 30mph before haring down the 1 in 172/228 to Southwaite at 90mph and 92 on the 1 in 131 after Wreay. Net time for the 69.1 miles from Lancaster was 58½ minutes.

46221, again on the 1958 7.45am Euston *Caledonian*, passed Carnforth seven minutes late because of earlier delays and managed to recover the whole of the lost time in the 31.4 miles to Shap Summit! Grayrigg Summit was passed at the exceptional speed of 66½mph which involved 2,150edbhp power output only 100 less than *Duchess of Abercorn's* 1939 epic test runs. This clearly did not wind the pacific for it tore away to 83½ before Tebay and assaulted Shap clearing the summit at 51mph, having covered the 18.6 uphill miles from Oxenholme in 16 minutes 5 seconds at an average speed of 69mph. A run timed by George Carpenter (our 'guru' from the Bevils Club, a group of railway engineers and authors meeting each Thursday lunchtime at the Institute of Civil Engineers in Westminster) of 46247 *City of Liverpool* on the 295 ton gross *Royal Scot* was even more astonishing. It had a good start, passing Carnforth at 82mph, Oxenholme at 60 and Grayrigg Summit at 57, then after 84 at Tebay, didn't fall below 60mph on the climb to Shap. It descended from Shap in a hurry, passing Clifton at 84 again, and after a p-way restriction to 30mph at Penrith, raced away again to 83 at Southwaite. The climb to Shap required the supreme effort on the 1 in 75 with an estimated power output of 2,600edbhp, way above that achieved by 46225 on Rugby Testing Plant and the prewar record. The 69.1 miles from Lancaster started at 72mph to the Carlisle stop was accomplished in no more than 57½ minutes net – at an average of 72.1mph.

A Birmingham-Glasgow/ Edinburgh train hauled by 46241 *City of Edinburgh* passed Lancaster 11½ minutes late but had also recouped the whole of that lost time by Shap Summit despite a signal stop between Carnforth and Milnthorpe. The train load was 382/405 tons and the highlights were a recovery to 76mph at Hincaster Junction, 62 at Oxenholme, a minimum of 48½mph at Grayrigg, 77 at Tebay and 37mph at Shap Summit. Carlisle was reached in 68 minutes 53 seconds for the 69.1 miles from Lancaster including the signal stand and a p-way restriction at Southwaite. Power outputs on the two banks were 1,750 and 1,860edbhp respectively. Then to compare with a heavier load, 46228 *Duchess of Rutland* had 524/570 tons on the *Midday Scot*, and after a signal check before Carnforth accelerated to 68mph at Milnthorpe and held 34mph on Grayrigg. From 64mph at Tebay, speed gradually fell to 30mph at Shap Summit, an effort that required a maximum of 2,360edbhp on the climb.

The *Midday Scot* was regularly 450-550 tons, one of the hardest turns, with just 80 minutes allowed for the 82.6 miles to Rugby and an easier 77 minutes for the 75.5 miles on to Crewe. Whilst normally hauled by a Duchess, there were occasional forays by a 'Princess Royal' and for a long period the BR 1954 built 8P *Duke of Gloucester* was rostered to this turn to Crewe. Between 1954 and 1958 Mr K.R.Phillips analysed a number of logs compiled by himself and friends of this train to its Rugby stop.

Class	No. of runs	Average gross load	Average net time
Duchess	18	457 tons	79.8 minutes
Princess Royal	9	439 tons	81.5 minutes
8P 71000	7	488 tons	83.2 minutes

This is not particularly impressive, since these are net times. In fact, only two trains from this set actually arrived at Rugby on time. Some recovered time on the easier timing on to Crewe. 46248 *City of Leeds* arrived with 510 tons in 78 min 53 secs (net 77½), and 46224 *Princess Alexandra* with 560 tons in 79 min 38 secs (76½ net). The latter topped Tring summit at 68mph, touched 84mph at Cheddington, was slowed to 32mph at Leighton Buzzard by a p-way check, cleared Roade at an excellent 71½mph and had further 80s at Blisworth, Weedon and Hillmorton. The best Princess Royal was 46212 *Duchess of Kent* in 81 min 03 secs (and the fastest net time of all in 74½ minutes) but with a considerably lighter train of just 390 tons. None of the *Duke of Gloucester* runs achieved a net time of less than 80 minutes.

Whilst the heavy overnight trains were rarely logged, one Duchess run that was recorded was of a Euston-Glasgow sleeper that was routed north of Carlisle via the Glasgow & South Western Railway route. A restaurant car was attached at Carlisle to provide breakfasts and on this occasion a late start caused by delays in the south gave the driver an incentive to run hard.

Dumfries-Kilmarnock

46249 *City of Sheffield* -Polmadie

14 chs, 532/555 tons

Euston-Glasgow sleeping car express

Miles	Location	Times	Speeds	Mins recovered	Gradients
0	Dumfries	00.00			
3.4	Holywood	06.06	58½		L
7.5	Auldgirth	10.23	54		1/200 R
11.45	Closeburn	14.12	63		L, 1/200 R
14.15	Thornhill	16.56	57½	1	1/150 R
17.5	Carronbridge	20.34	53/64½		1/150 R, 1/200 F
26.1	Sanquhar	29.18	51	3¾	1/180 R
29.45	Kirkconnel	33.10	pws 35*/62		L
36.9	New Cumnock	43.30	pws 40*	2½	L
42.25	Cumnock	50.14	59*		1/146 F
44.25	Auchinleck	52.10	65		L
48.65	Mauchline	56.08	67	1	1/150 F, L
51.4	Garrochburn	58.35	79		1/100 F
56.3	Hurlford	62.51	60*		
<u>58.05</u>	<u>Kilmarnock</u>	<u>65.36</u>	(net 61 ½)	<u>4½</u>	

46249 then climbed the five miles to Stewarton – 1 in 180, followed by 1 in 87 and finally a 1½ mile stretch of 1 in 75 after Stewarton to the summit at MP 17 before Dunlop at 38 – 42mph, falling to 36 on the 1 in 75, gaining another minute on schedule and despite signal checks outside St Enoch, picked up a couple of minutes on the last section. Cecil J. Allen experienced a run over this route in the autumn of 1961 on the 11.40pm Euston-Glasgow sleeper, which had been hauled by a class 40 diesel electric locomotive to Carlisle and was replaced there by Polmadie's 46230 *Duchess of Buccleuch*. It had a load of 13 coaches, 493/515 tons, and was facing appalling weather, pouring rain and a wild westerly gale. It took just ¾ minute more to pass Carronbridge with speeds of 54 at Auldgirth, 60 at Closeburn and 47 at Carronbridge and with a p-way slowing at Kirkconnel to 25mph and another after Mauchline to 25 also, took 69 minutes 25 seconds to Kilmarnock, excellent in the prevailing stormy conditions.

Whilst the night sleepers were rarely timed (although in chapter 5, Driver Les Jackson describes a footplate journey on one of them when he was the fireman), the Duchesses were sometimes utilised for fill-in trips to Dundee or Aberdeen during the day lay-over at Perth. Three run logs were quoted by Cecil J. Allen with 46229, 46233 and 46235 when with 10 coach 320 ton gross trains they covered the relatively flat 32½ miles between Forfar and Perth in around 30 minutes net with sustained running in the low 80s, but this was easy compared with the night work.

The Duchesses did not always cope well in wet conditions. A comment in the 1955 Rugby Test Plant report about the test being limited by 46225's slipping was echoed in a *Railway Magazine* article by Cecil J. Allen in 1963, referring back to a footplate run he had had with 46225 *Duchess of Gloucester* also. To quote, '…my own personal records, made on the footplate, and while travelling many times in heavy Anglo-Scottish expresses, contain an uncomfortable number of occasions when the effectiveness of these engines was severely limited by their liability to slip.' He then described the footplate run he had with 46225 on the Down *Midday Scot* and 530 tons gross on a raw winter's day with intermittent showers. They were going well enough to Carnforth until brought almost to a stand at the beginning of the 1 in 111 a couple of miles before Oxenholme. The driver then had great difficulty in getting 46225 to grip the rails and took over nine minutes to reach Oxenholme station where a decision was made to await a banker. A 2-6-4T was found and the pair eventually got the *Midday Scot* running at 40mph on the climb to Grayrigg, losing some twenty minutes in running as a result. O.S. Nock had a similar experience in 1959 with an unnamed Duchess. Despite passing Beattock at speed, they took 28 minutes to reach the summit with prolonged and repeated slipping and water supply was so depleted that they had to stop at the summit to fill the tender, thus taking over two and a half hours for the 102 miles from Carlisle to Glasgow. And in 1959 a Duchess spent an hour trying to start the 500 ton *Red Rose* out of Liverpool Lime Street before the embarrassed driver succeeded!

A spectacular run on the Up *Caledonian* was made on 5 September 1957 when 46244 *King George VI* and its 8-coach train arrived at Euston 37 minutes early! Apparently, official permission had been given to Driver Starvis of Camden to attempt an exceptionally fast run – a 15 minute early arrival at Euston was requested to test the feasibility of accelerating the *Caledonian*. Unfortunately, there was no recorder on the train to take detailed times and speeds but outline times and speeds were calculated. The 299.1 miles from Carlisle to Euston were completed in 253 minutes (242 net) – average speed 70.9mph (74.1 net). The train sped out of Carlisle almost attaining even time on the uphill grades to Plumpton, 12.8 miles, but the signalman at Penrith was not ready for a train that was already six minutes early. After a 3-minute stand, Shap summit was passed 4 minutes early in 35 minutes for the 31.4 miles (29 net) and after braking to 68mph at Oxenholme, touched 100 at Hincaster Junction, averaging 90mph from Oxenholme to Carnforth. After a p-way slack at Lancaster and a signal check at Norton Crossing, Crewe was passed 13 minutes early. The 158.1 miles from Crewe took exactly two hours, just one minute more than the 1937 *Coronation Scot* press run. 100mph was reached at three further locations – Castlethorpe, King's Langley and Wembley. Tring summit was cleared at around 91-92mph – the Bletchley-Tring average was 93.3mph. The 54½ miles from Roade to Willesden Junction were run at an average of

92mph. Driver Starvis claimed that 46244 was the 'pick of a very good bunch' and it does seem to have been recorded on a number of good runs in that period along with sister 46245 *City of London*. Doug Landau calculated 1,700edbhp was needed to clear Tring summit at this speed – 2,600ihp. The fireman on this heroic run was John Tumilty of Camden, who had fired a lot of soft Scottish coal into the firebox during the 299 mile run. Goodness knows what the passengers made of this run. There is no record of whether the speed caused undue discomfort in the train – or more to the point, in the restaurant car – and the only reaction recorded was a comment in the John Clay/Joseph Cliffe book that one passenger jumped out of the train before it came to a stand and sprinted for the Underground, throwing a withering look at the engine and crew!

1957 and 1958 seem to have been good years for the Duchesses, the last years when steam reigned supreme before the influx of main line diesels began. A large number of logs for Duchess runs have surfaced for those years. Camden's 46242 was a regular performer on the *Caledonian* during its first month of running in June and a couple of logs for the Up journey with this engine are shown below. The first on 18 June departed 6½ minutes late and the second which was timed from Glasgow left Carlisle just a minute late. The Glasgow-Carlisle 107 minute schedule for the 102.3 miles was completed on time on this run (102 minutes net), with 77mph at Lamington, 55 minimum at Beattock and 83 at Kirkpatrick. Driver Young from Camden took over there.

Carlisle-Preston
46242 *City of Glasgow*
8 chs, 264/285 tons
The Caledonian

		18.6.1957			27.6.1957			
Miles	Location	Times	Speeds		Times	Speeds		Gradients
0	Carlisle	00.00		6½ L	00.00		1 L	
	Wreay	-	48		-			
13.1	Plumpton	-	pws 25*		17.56	64/70		1 L 1/131 R, 1/172 R, L
17.8	Penrith	22.05	70	5½ L	22.06	74	T	
	Eden Valley Jn	-	75		-	80		L
	Clifton & Lowther	-	65		-	69		1/125 R
	Thrimby Grange	-	62		-	56		1/125 R
29.4	Shap	-	57/61		32.47	54/60		1/125 R, L
31.4	Shap Summit	34.44	58	2¼ L	34.57	55	3 E	1/106 R, 1/130 R
	Scout Green	-			-	78		1/75 F
36.9	Tebay	38.57	84½	½ L	39.37	pws 25*	4½ E	L
50	Oxenholme	48.55	75*	1½ E	53.49	75	2¼ E	1/131 F
	Hincaster Junction	-			-	pws 25*		
62.8	Carnforth	58.40	90	2¾ E	66.54	78/74	T	1/134 F
	Hest Bank	-	84		-	78		L
69.1	Lancaster	63.17	74½	3¼ E	71.57	72	T	
80.6	Garstang	73.21	72½	3¼ E	81.20	85	¾ E	L
90	Preston	83.00	34*	3½ E	87.34	55*	1½ E	

The recorder on the first run continued timing south of Preston. Crewe (141.1 miles) was passed in 140 minutes 10 seconds, 7¾ minutes early, and key features thereafter were 88mph at Norton Bridge, 83 before Lichfield, a p-way slowing to 25mph between Nuneaton and Rugby, 83½ at Weedon, 68 minimum at Roade, 85 at Castlethorpe, 72mph minimum at Tring, 85 at King's Langley and 83½ at Wembley. Arrival was 5½ minutes early at Euston in 279 minutes 5 seconds (269 minutes net) for the 299.1 miles.

46244 was timed by H.G. Ellison on the Down *Caledonian* on 25 September 1957 and it passed Crewe seven minutes early despite a 10mph p-way slack at Wembley and a signal check approaching Crewe. The driver was Spencer of Camden and the load the usual 264/280 tons. Watford Junction was passed a minute late at 73mph and after falling to 68 at Hemel Hempstead, 46244 actually accelerated to 74mph at Tring summit. Even time was reached by Bletchley after 81mph at Cheddington and then 84 at Wolverton was followed by a minimum of 72 at Roade, the train now on time. Rugby was passed in just under 75 minutes 'two minutes early' and sustained speed of 82-84mph made the train six minutes early passing Lichfield. A short burst of 84mph at Betley Road before the Crewe check and the station was passed at 15mph in 139 minutes from London. Up to 80 by Winsford and despite signal checks at Warrington to 40mph and a p-way slack at Wigan to 35mph, Preston was passed 8½ minutes early. 46244 was then eased to avoid excessive early running but 52mph at Grayrigg and 39 at Shap summit had increased the earliness to ten minutes. Easy running with nothing over 75mph then brought the *Caledonian* into Carlisle eight minutes early in 278 minutes net or nearer 272 minutes had the train continued from Shap at the normal high speed.

Both 46242 and 46244 seem to have been frequently employed on these 8-coach flyers. Lt Alcock timed 46242 in November 1959 on the *Royal Scot* north of the border when it left Carlisle 24 minutes late after a succession of signal checks north of Lancaster. It then regained four of those minutes by achieving 92½mph after Lockerbie, passing Beattock, 39.8 miles in 34 minutes at 79, and clearing Beattock Summit, 49.8 miles in 44½ minutes at 57mph.

In June 1958 the Rev R.S. Haines treated himself to a week of travelling on the *Caledonian* both ways between Carlisle and Euston and back again – could you buy a weekly season ticket from Carlisle to Euston? He possibly used an LM Region Rail Rover ticket. With the introduction of the second *Caledonian* service, he could have left London at 7.45am and returned the same day, but he chose to stay overnight in Carlisle and commence his daily journey from there. I table below a summary of all ten runs to show the consistency of running and the apparent reserve the Duchesses had showing the net gains on the 291 minute schedule for the 299.1 miles.

Up *Caledonian* 10.15am Carlisle – Euston, 8 chs, 16 June 1958 – 20 June 1958

| | | | 46239 | 46257 | 46239 | 46245 | 46241 |
| | | | 16/6 | 17/6 | 18/6 | 19/6 | 20/6 |
Miles	Location	Sch	Times	Times	Times	Times	Times
17.9	Penrith	23	20.10	19.21	21.42	19.46	21.41
31.4	Shap Summit	39	34.03	33.24	35.10	33.40	36.30
62.8	Carnforth	68	61.52	59.43	68.24*	60.24	62.43
69.1	Lancaster	73	73.27*	68.27	74.55	67.25	69.21
90.1	Preston	93	97.08**	90.55**	98.07**	88.23**	90.05**
141	Crewe	148	152.07	143.24	153.50	145.18	150.33*
216.5	Rugby	219	226.46	214.12	227.00	214.49	219.17
299.1	Euston	291	295.03	294.56*	299.10	285.29	287.38
Net times:				277 ¼	275	278 ¼	268 ½	271 ¼

Down *Caledonian* 4.15pm Euston – Carlisle, 8 chs, 16 June 1958 – 20 June 1958

			46257	46239	46245	46241	46248
			16/6	17/6	18/6	19/6	20/6
Miles	Location	Sch	Times	Times	Times	Times	Times
82.6	Rugby	77	73.52	75.27	73.28	76.18	72.44
158.1	Crewe	146	144.42	143.12	138.24	142.04	141.52
209	Preston	202	199.50	201.30**	193.15	194.12	199.21
236.6	Carnforth	227	227.36**	229.00	222.51	226.55	229.42*
262.2	Tebay	254	252.46	252.24	249.03	245.12	256.27*
267.7	Shap Summit	262	259.28	258.34	256.29	252.07	263.12
299.1	Carlisle	291	288.49	289.44	286.23	281.42	292.54*
Net times:			281 ½	285 ½	279 ½	277 ¾	275 ½

Notes: * signal checks in section
        ** p-way restrictions in section

The Camden engine and crew would travel north, lodge overnight and return the next morning. I'm unsure if the slight variations in performance reflect different crews or that of the locomotive. Most crew links would vary during the week rather than repeat the diagram each day. 46245 certainly had a good reputation at that time. Although 46239 appears the 'weakest' of the five, its time from Carnforth to Shap Summit on 17 June was the fastest, and the 5 miles from Tebay to Shap Summit, at 6 minutes 10 seconds, also the fastest. In the Down direction only, the last run was late, incurred entirely by signal checks approaching Carlisle. In the Up direction, all the runs lost time on the approaches to Preston because of p-way checks and the first three finished 4-8 minutes late, the last two arriving early with significantly faster net times. No speeds were quoted in these logs, but a couple of other logs for the Down additional *Caledonian* with the Polmadie Duchesses, quoted 46231 *Duchess of Atholl* with 60mph minimum at Grayrigg and 57 at Shap, whilst 46232 *Duchess of Montrose* was timed at 59mph at Grayrigg and 54½ at Shap.

The Rail Performance Society has a number of runs of both the *Caledonian* and the 8-coach *Royal Scot* – all the Anglo-Scottish day trains including the *Midday Scot* were limited to eight coaches from 1960. I've chosen a couple where the engine and crew stuck closely to the schedule to show what was required from the Duchesses to keep time. 46240 *City of Coventry* was recorded on the northbound *Royal Scot* in December 1960 – nothing spectacular, but what could be expected day in, day out. North of the border a similar 'normal' run, with Camden's old favourite, 46245 *City of London*, again.

Preston-Carlisle

46240 *City of Coventry*

8 chs, 274/290 tons

The Royal Scot

14.12.1960

Miles	Location	Times	Speeds		Gradients
0	Preston	00.00		T	
9.5	Garstang	11.33	74		L
21	Lancaster	21.08	67*	1 L	
	Hest Bank	-	77		
27.4	Carnforth	26.07	72	1¼ L	

Preston-Carlisle

46240 *City of Coventry*

8 chs, 274/290 tons

The Royal Scot

14.12.1960

Miles	Location	Times	Speeds		Gradients
34.7	Milnthorpe	-	60/70		1/134 R/ L
40.1	Oxenholme	38.18	52	1¼ L	1/111 R
43.6	Hay Fell	-	45		1/131 R
47.2	Grayrigg	47.43	42/69		1/106 R
53.2	Tebay	53.24	67		L
56.2	Scout Green	-	54		1/75 R (heavy mist)
58.7	Shap summit	59.44	40/49	T	1/75 R
68	Clifton	-	65/73		1/125 F
72.2	Penrith	72.08	63*	¼ L	
77	Plumpton	76.07	80	T	1/131 F
90.1	Carlisle	88.38		½ E	

Carlisle-Glasgow Central

46245 *City of London* - Camden

8 chs, 280/295 tons

10 June 1960

The Caledonian

Driver Messenger, Upperby

Miles	Location	Times	Speeds		Gradients
0	Carlisle	00.00	sigs 15*	T	
8.6	Gretna Junction	10.43	80/76	¾ L	L
13	Kirkpatrick	14.20	71		1/200 R
16	Kirtlebridge	17.21	79		1/190 F, L
22.6	Castlemilk Sdgs	-	pws 50*/70		1/200 R
25.8	Lockerbie	26.15	sigs 35*	2¼ L	1/528 F
34.5	Wamphray	34.30	74		1/330 F
39.7	Beattock	39.00	68	3 L	1/202 R
	Greskine	-	41		1/74 R
	Harthope	-	36		1/69R
49.7	Beattock Summit	52.17	43/46	2¼ L	1/74 R

Carlisle-Glasgow Central

46245 *City of London* - Camden

8 chs, 280/295 tons

10 June 1960

The Caledonian

Driver Messenger, Upperby

Miles	Location	Times	Speeds		Gradients
52.6	Elvanfoot	54.49	83/70*		1/99 F
63.2	Lamington	63.50	63*/79		1/294 F, L
73.6	Carstairs	72.26	50*	½ E	
	Carlike	-	76		1/98 F
84.1	Law Junction	82.19	45*	1¾ E	1/140 F
89.5	Motherwell	89.21	pws 25*/sigs 35*	1½ E	1/116 F
	Uddingston	-	pws 20*		1/135 F
	Newton	-	sigs 50*/pws 20*		
102.3	Glasgow Central	107.49	(100 net)	¾ L	

The *Caledonian* was decelerated by twenty-five minutes in 1959 and a further ten in 1960 because of increasing electrification works south of Crewe. To show the impact of the electrification work on Duchess pacific performance, I will show below the full log of the Up *Caledonian* from Carlisle just before Christmas 1960. A normal seven minute recovery time was inserted in the schedule between Carlisle and Crewe, but no less than 41 minutes between Crewe and Euston. A 13-minute dead stand signal check halfway down Beattock bank and further signal checks caused the train to leave Carlisle 25¾ minutes late. The recovery time enabled a 4¼ minute early arrival.

Glasgow-Euston

The Caledonian

46245 *City of London* – Camden

8 chs, 280/295 tons

21.2.1960

Miles	Location	Times	Speeds		Gradients
0	Glasgow Central	00.00		T	
28.5	Carstairs	44.41	sigs from M'well	5¾ L	
35.5	Symington	52.06	75		
44.5	Abington	60.32	65		1/294 R
47.1	Crawford	63.06	61		1/240 R
49.75	Elvanfoot	65.56	56		L, 1/99 R
52.65	Beattock Summit	69.17	52/81	7¼ L	1/75 F

Glasgow-Euston

The Caledonian

46245 *City of London* – Camden

8 chs, 280/295 tons

21.2.1960

Miles	Location	Times	Speeds		Gradients	
	Greskine	76.22/89.03	sig stand		1/75 F	
62.65	Beattock	93.15	80	21¼ L	1/88 F	
	Wamphray	-	85		1/202 F	
	Dinwoodie	-	78/87		1/330 R, 1/326 F	
	Nethercleugh	-	76/86			
	Lockerbie	104.25	73/82	20¼ L	1/200 R, 1/200 F	
	Kirtlebridge	-	74/76			
93.65	Gretna Junction	119.36	68/76	21½ L	1/200 F	
102.25	Carlisle	130.18	sigs	23¼ L		
0		00.00		25¾ L		
	Wreay	-	41/48		1/131 R	
	Calthwaite	-	58/63		1/228 R, 1/172 R	
12.95	Plumpton	16.04	73	23¾ L		
17.85	Penrith	20.05	69	22¾ L		
	Thrimby Grange	-	68/63		1/125 R	
	Shap	-	64/61/64		1/125 R, L	
31.55	Shap Summit	32.29	61	19¼ L	1/106 R	
37	Tebay	37.26	74/sigs	18 L		
42.95	Grayrigg	43.13	sigs 23*		1/106 F	
50	Oxenholme	50.46	76	19½ L	1/178 F	
	Milnthorpe	-	84		1/173 F	
62.85	Carnforth	61.39	76	19¼ L		
	Hest Bank	-	80		L	
69.1	Lancaster	67.33	61*	20¼ L		
	Scorton	-	82		L	
80.6	Garstang	77.48	78/83	20½ L	L	
90.1	Preston	87.13	20*	19¾ L		
	Euxton Junction	95.17	sigs 10*	21 L		[3] recovery time
105.2	Wigan	107.00	60	18¾ L		
116.9	Warrington	119.42	67/48*	19¼ L		

Glasgow-Euston

The Caledonian

46245 *City of London* – **Camden**

8 chs, 280/295 tons

21.2.1960

Miles	Location	Times	Speeds	Gradients		
	Hartford	-	81	L		
132.3	Winsford Junction	134.30	74/80		1/300 R, L	[4]
141.1	Crewe	143.37	20*	16½ L		
	Crewe South	147.34/148.00 sig stand				
151.45	Whitmore	159.59	56/67	21¾ L		
	Norton Bridge	-	81/78			[5]
165.5	Stafford	174.51	sigs 25*	19½ L		
	Colwich	182.06/182.26 sig stand				[5]
174.8	Rugeley	190.47	76	21¾ L		
182.85	Lichfield	197.23	86	22 L	1/331 F	
189.1	Tamworth	202.04	78/82	20¾ L	1/359 R	
	Atherstone	-	sigs 55*			[5]
202	Nuneaton	213.44	63/75	15½ L		
	Brinklow	-	85	L		[5]
216.55	Rugby	227.16	sigs 25*	10 L		
220.7	Kilsby	232.21	61/53		1/370 R	[5]
229.4	Weedon	239.27	81	6 L	1/350 F	
236.25	Blisworth	245.07	68/77	6¾ L	L	
239.2	Roade	247.42	69	6¼ L	1/320 R	
	Castlethorpe	-	81		1/326 F	[5]
246.7	Wolverton	253.46	pws 40*			
252.45	Bletchley	261.43	53/79	4¼ L		
265.15	Tring	274.31	65	4¼ L	1/333 R	
	Hemel Hempstead	-	85/72		1/335 F	[5]
281.65	Watford Junction	286.52	60/76	1½ L		
287.7	Harrow & Wealdstone	291.58	67/76			[5]
293.7	Willesden Junction	297.17	54*/68	4 E		[1]
299.1	Euston	305.59		4¼ E		

In a performance evaluation by John Powell of the Derby Motive Power team, a calculation was made that a Duchess, provided with a mechanical stoker and performing at the level demonstrated in the Rugby Test Plant with 46225, could achieve a time of 138 minutes for the 158.1 miles to Crewe with 550 tons. This would require full regulator and 25 per cent cut-off on the long 1 in 330 gradients and 22 per cent cut-off elsewhere and envisaged 66mph minimum at Tring, 70 at Roade and maximum speeds of 83 at Cheddington, 81 at Nuneaton, 82 at Hademore and 86 at Betley Road. This would mean with some recovery time that a cut of ten minutes in the best XL timings could be achieved. However, such calculation with the necessary investment in a mechanical stoker system and appropriate trials came too late. The English Electric 2,000 hp diesels were arriving in force, although their maximum edbhp was in the region of 1,350 only, well short of the power a Duchess could produce. Interestingly, a comparison had been made in 1957 with the running of one of the prototype diesel electrics, 10203, which worked originally on the Southern Region and was transferred to Camden to join 10000 and 10001 along with the other slightly less powerful 10201 and 10202. With a 13-coach 435/470 ton load on the *Midday Scot* Rugby was reached in 83 minutes 8 seconds (net 80½) – a loss of half a minute net on the schedule but similar in many ways to some of the run of the mill but poorer runs recorded by Mr Phillips and quoted earlier. Tring summit was cleared at 61mph, and Roade at 63, but the highest maximum speed was only 75mph near Blisworth.

The Duchesses were averaging 70-75,000 miles per annum in the 1950s and their mileages between Intermediate or General Works repairs were on the whole better than most other 8P classes, averaging around 90,000 miles in the later 1950s (discounting casual repairs in between). The English based Duchesses averaged higher mileages between Works than the Scottish engines, partly as the latter took longer to assemble mileage as their diagrams involved shorter turns, mostly confined to Scotland. As examples I show below some mileages of engines between major overhauls selected at random:

	English based Duchesses			Polmadie based Duchesses		
	46237	46244	46245	46223	46231	46232
1952/3	96,768	99,331	36,384	78,223	58,477	63,160
1954/5	103,477	86,959	104,056	77,688	67,088	50,143
1956/7	89,539	108,988	92,977	80,715	89,271	61,827
1958/9	97,696	97,613	98,809	92,519	87,461	59,861
1960/1	110,544	93,291	94,518	80,007	76,195	90,428

	H.G.Ivatt 1947 build	
	46256	46257
1952/3	89,863	75,084
1954/5	156,065	142,486 (both after two 'casuals')
1956/7	100,590	96,641
1958/9	93,594	83,621
1960/1	88,073	84,179

46245 had a succession of Works visits in the 1951-3 period and 46232 seems to have had a poor record in particular, except the final 1959-60 period when its activity seems to have been more trouble free. Although the Ivatt engines were designed specifically to achieve longer mileages between Works repairs, they do not seem to have been markedly better than the other English based Duchesses apart from a period from 1953-5 when their mileages were extended by intermediate casual Works repairs, although it is not known if this was planned experimentally or caused by failures or damage necessitating Works attention.

Ex-works 46242 *City of Glasgow* running in on the 5.53pm Manchester London Road to Crewe at Burnage, 24 April 1957. (R. Gee/MLS Collection)

Camden's 46242 *City of Glasgow* speeds the *Caledonian* through Hest Bank, Summer 1957. (MLS Collection)

26 • THE LMS PRINCESS CORONATION PACIFICS, THE FINAL YEARS & PRESERVATION

46242 *City of Glasgow* leaving Primrose Hill Tunnel and beginning the descent of Camden Bank with the *Caledonian*, Summer 1957.
(MLS Collection)

46239 *City of Chester* arriving at Euston on the *Caledonian*, 1958. On the extreme left of the photo is a 'Jinty' tank waiting to propel a set of coaches into the station.
(P.H. Groom/MLS Collection)

46254 *City* of Stoke-on-Trent on the Up *Royal Scot* south of Bletchley, c1957. (Photomatic/MLS Collection)

46257 *City* of Salford with the *Royal Scot* in the Preston area, c1957. (Arthur Bendall/MLS Collection)

28 • THE LMS PRINCESS CORONATION PACIFICS, THE FINAL YEARS & PRESERVATION

46225 *Duchess of Gloucester* at Elvanfoot with the 17-coach 9.25am Glasgow/Edinburgh-Birmingham, 30 June 1957.
(R.E. Gee/MLS Collection)

46240 *City of Coventry* climbing to Shap Summit, coal-pusher operating, with the Down *Royal Scot*, 5 September 1957.
(P.H. Groom/MLS Collection)

Polmadie's 46232 *Duchess of Montrose* on the second *Caledonian* service introduced in the summer of 1958, the 7.45am from Euston, seen at Dillicar, August 1958. (M.L. Boakes/MLS Collection)

46229 *Duchess of Hamilton* draws into Wigan North West station with an express watched by a boy in standard trainspotter's outfit of the fifties, 7 June 1958. (R. Farrell/MLS Collection)

46240 *City* *of Coventry* passes the trainspotters' favourite location, Tamworth, at speed with an Up express, c1958. (MLS Collection)

Carlisle trainspotters consult their Ian Allan ABCs as Polmadie's *46232 Duchess of Montrose* gives way to Crewe's 46234 *Duchess of Abercorn* on a Glasgow – Euston express, 1958. (MLS Collection)

46244 *King* George VI at Winwick Quay with the 10.5am Glasgow-Birmingham, 27 December 1958.
(MLS Collection)

46229 *Duchess of Hamilton* arriving on the 9.35am Euston *Comet* at Manchester London Road, 27 February 1959.
(MLS Collection)

Next morning
Camden's 46229 *Duchess of Hamilton* is about to depart on the Up *Mancunian* from Manchester London Road, 28 February 1959.
(MLS Collection)

46238 *City of Carlisle* near Euxton Junction with the Up *Royal Scot*, 11 April 1959.
(R. Farrell/MLS Collection)

46234 *Duchess of Abercorn* with a Birmingham-Glasgow express between Balshaw and Leyland, 11 April 1959. (R. Farrell/MLS Collection)

46250 *City of Lichfield* at Shap with the Saturday heavier *Royal Scot*, 17 May 1959. (E.R. Morten/MLS Collection)

34 • THE LMS PRINCESS CORONATION PACIFICS, THE FINAL YEARS & PRESERVATION

46226 *Duchess of Norfolk* powers through Leyland with an Up express, 23 May 1959. (R. Farrell/MLS Collection)

46231 *Duchess of Atholl* passing Hest Bank with the Up *Midday Scot*, 20 June 1959. (R. Farrell/MLS Collection)

1957–60 • 35

46241 *City* of *Edinburgh* at Ashton with the Up *Royal Scot*, 7 August 1959. (L. Hanson/MLS Collection)

46221 *Queen* Elizabeth at Thrimby Grange on the southbound climb to Shap with the 9am Perth-Euston, 18 July 1959. (A.C. Gilbert/MLS Collection)

46240 *City of Coventry* departing southbound from Crewe near Betley Road with the Up *Royal Scot,* 8 August 1959. (A.C. Gilbert/MLS Collection)

46245 *City of London* on the Up *Caledonian* at Madeley, 4 September 1959. (R. Farrell/MLS Collection)

46237 *City of Bristol* climbing from Farington to Leyland with an Up Perth-Euston express, 20 September 1958. (MLS Collection)

46255 *City of Hereford* passing Edge Hill with the Up *Merseyside Express*, 21 May 1958. (R. Hewitt/ MLS Collection)

46230 *Duchess of Buccleuch* has stopped at Beattock station for a banker and is just departing with a Glasgow bound express, 1 August 1959. (P. Hutchinson/MLS Collection)

46252 *City of Leicester* is turning on a triangle from Stockport at Davenport Junction, on the Buxton line, after the removal of the 70ft turntable at Manchester London Road, 21 June 1958. The 60ft turntable at Longsight could not handle any visiting pacifics. (MLS Collection)

Chapter 3
THE FINAL YEARS, 1960–1964

The summer timetable of 1960 had 26 daytime main line departures from Euston for Crewe and the north and three from Birmingham and there were 14 night services of which 12 had sleeping cars (see appendix, pages 174 and 175). Before the growth of domestic air services, there were six services for Ireland via Holyhead, Heysham and Stranraer. Most of the regular and heaviest West Coast expresses were in the hands of the English Electric Class 40s, especially south of Crewe and on the Liverpool and Manchester expresses, where much of the electrification work was in progress. The overnight sleeping car trains to and from Glasgow, Edinburgh, Perth, Oban and Inverness were however mainly in the hands of Crewe North and Carlisle Upperby Duchesses. The 8-coach *Caledonian*, *Royal Scot* and *Midday Scot* were steam hauled until dieselised in 1962. The allocation of Duchesses in the summer of 1960 stood as follows:

Camden:	46239, 46240, 46242, 46243, 46245-46247 (7)
Crewe:	46220, 46221, 46228, 46229, 46235, 46241, 46248, 46249, 46251, 46253, 46254, 46256 (12)
Edge Hill:	46233
Carlisle Upperby:	46225, 46226, 46234, 46236-46238, 46244, 46250, 46252, 46255, 46257 (11)
Polmadie:	46222-46224, 46227, 46230-46232 (7)

It will be noted from the above that the Duchess work was now concentrated north of Crewe, especially on the Crewe-Carlisle section where the extra power of the Duchesses was most critical, especially on the heavy overnight sleeper services. Many of these hard turns were rarely recorded. However, 46244 *King George VI* was timed on the 16-coach 9.50pm Perth-Euston.

Carlisle-Crewe

46244 *King George VI* – Carlisle Upperby

16 chs, 595/620 tons

9.50pm Perth – Euston sleeper

17.8.1963

Miles	Location	Times	Speeds		Gradients
0	Carlisle	00.00		T	
7.3	Southwaite	15.27			1/131 R
13.1	Plumpton	23.41	52		1/172 R
17.8	Penrith	29.26	60		

Carlisle-Crewe

46244 *King George VI* – Carlisle Upperby

16 chs, 595/620 tons

9.50pm Perth – Euston sleeper

17.8.1963

Miles	Location	Times	Speeds	Gradients
	Thrimby Grange	-	34/32	1/125 R
	Shap	46.57	37/42	1/125 R, L
31.4	Shap Summit	50.10	38	1/106 R, 1/130 R
36.9	Tebay	55.38	76	1/75 F, L
43	Grayrigg	61.18	56 eased	
50	Oxenholme	67.38	78	1/131 F
	Hincaster Junction	70.21	83	1/173 F
62.8	Carnforth	78.25	64	
	Hest Bank	-	61	L
69.1	Lancaster	84.51	55*	
80.6	Garstang	96.09	73	L
90	Preston	106.27	33* / sigs 8*	
105.2	Wigan	132.53	62	
117	Warrington	145.34	55*	
124.8	Weaver Junction	153.30	63	
	Hartford	-	66/70	
	Coal Yard Jn	-	sigs	
<u>141</u>	<u>Crewe</u>	<u>173.50</u>		<u>8 E</u>

46247 *City of Liverpool* at Leeds City with the RCTS railtour to Carlisle, July 1961. (G.W. Sharpe/MLS Collection)

The Duchesses began to be selected for railtours from 1960 onwards as it became more difficult to guarantee what services they might haul amongst the diesels. The RCTS ran a special on the Settle & Carlisle line in 1961 and had 46247 *City of Liverpool* on 10 coaches, 355 tons gross. It was taken easily down to Settle Junction, passed at 66mph, and was then opened out, holding 60 ½mph on the 1 in 100 at Horton–in-Ribblesdale and 56½ at Ribblehead, passing Blea Moor (17.3 miles) in 18 minutes 45 seconds from the Hellifield start. 2,200edbhp was registered during this climb. There was then Sunday engineering work involving single line working between Dent and Garsdale, followed by easy running in the low 70s down to Appleby and a final fling at 83mph at Lazonby before a succession of signal checks were encountered all the way to Carlisle.

The Final Years, 1960–1964 • 41

46244 *King* George VI running in after overhaul at Crewe Works on the 1.5pm Liverpool-Crewe stopping train at Acton Bridge, 18 June 1960.
(J. Hilton/MLS Collection)

46252 *City* of Leicester on the turntable of its home depot, Carlisle Kingmoor, c1962.
(MLS Collection)

42 • THE LMS PRINCESS CORONATION PACIFICS, THE FINAL YEARS & PRESERVATION

Polmadie's 46227
Duchess of Devonshire at Carlisle Citadel station returning to Kingmoor depot after release from a service from Glasgow, c1961. 46227 had a reputation of being the most 'reclusive' of the Polmadie Duchesses. It is therefore somewhat surprising that it was the author's first Duchess 'cop' on the *Royal Scot* at Euston in 1950.
(B.K.B. Green/MLS Collection)

Carlisle Upperby's
46234 *Duchess of Abercorn* passing Tamworth with the Down *Caledonian*, c1960.
(MLS Collection)

The Final Years, 1960–1964 • 43

Upperby's 46255 *City of Hereford* being banked out of Euston up Camden Bank with the Down *Caledonian*, 5 May 1960. (P.H. Groom/MLS Collection)

46242 *City of Glasgow* at Carlisle Citadel station with the Up *Caledonian*, 29 September 1960. (Brian Hilton/MLS Collection)

44 • THE LMS PRINCESS CORONATION PACIFICS, THE FINAL YEARS & PRESERVATION

Camden's 46246 *City of Manchester* at rest after arrival at Euston with an express, c1960. (MLS Collection)

46257 *City of Salford* shuts off steam as it eases an Up express near Wigan, c1960. (I. Vaughan/MLS Collection)

The Final Years, 1960–1964 • 45

46240 *City of Coventry* stands at Crewe with an Up express, while 'Black 5', 45142 awaits its turn of duty, c1960. (I. Vaughan/MLS Collection)

46236 *City of Bradford* on arrival at Euston with a West Coast express alongside an English Electric Type 4 (class 40) diesel electric, c1961. (M.L. Boakes & MLS Collections)

46 • THE LMS PRINCESS CORONATION PACIFICS, THE FINAL YEARS & PRESERVATION

Crimson red 46244 *King George VI* on the 10.5am Glasgow-Birmingham at Verdins, 8 August 1960. Note two ex-LNER coaches at the front. (J. Hilton/MLS Collection)

46245 *City of London* on the Saturday Up *Royal Scot* at Acton Bridge, 9 July 1960. (J. Hilton/MLS Collection)

The Final Years, 1960–1964 • 47

46249 *City of Sheffield* at Carlisle with a Glasgow-Birmingham express, a former Hawksworth GW coach at the front, c1960. 'Black 5', 45466, stands ready to return to Kingmoor shed. (A. Tyson/MLS Collection)

Camden's 46239 *City of Chester* climbs to Shap Summit with the Down *Shamrock Express* for Stranraer, c1961. (MLS Collection)

Polmadie's 46230 *Duchess of Buccleuch* with the 10.5am Glasgow-Birmingham, ex-GW coach at the front, at Preston Brook, 8 April 1961. (A.C. Gilbert/MLS Collection)

46225 *Duchess of Gloucester* climbs the gradient to Boar's Head with a Down express, 20 May 1961. (R. Farrell/MLS Collection)

The Final Years, 1960–1964 • 49

46246 *City of Manchester* passing Golbourne with the 10.15am semi-fast Glasgow-Euston train that followed the *Royal Scot*, 19 September 1961. Note the milk tank at the rear. (A.C. Gilbert/MLS Collection)

46247 *City of Liverpool* with the limited load Down *Royal Scot* at Winwick Junction, 18 March 1961. (A.C. Gilbert/MLS Collection)

46250 *City of Lichfield* passing through Wigan with the morning Glasgow-Birmingham express, 2 September 1961. (MLS Collection)

A panned shot of 46256 *Sir William A. Stanier FRS* at speed somewhere on the West Coast main line, c1962. (MLS Collection)

46226 *Duchess of Norfolk* at Carlisle with a Down express while station pilot 'Jinty' 47667 adds a van to the back of an Up train, 28 April 1962. (D.F. Tee/MLS Collection)

46241 *City* of Edinburgh hurries through Hartford with the morning Glasgow-Birmingham express, 13 April 1962. (J. Hilton/MLS Collection)

46253 *City of St Albans* at the head of an Up express, while V2 60802 and a Gresley V1 2-6-2T await duties over the line to Newcastle. (Photomatic/MLS Collection)

46254 *City of Stoke-on-Trent* runs into Stockport station with the Up *Comet*, 11 May 1962. (G. Coltas/MLS Collection)

The Final Years, 1960–1964 • 53

46256 *Sir William A. Stanier FRS* halts at Hartford with the 6.10am Carlisle-Crewe stopping train, 12 April 1962. (J. Hilton/MLS Collection)

46253 *City of St Albans* on the early morning Carlisle-Crewe stopping service at Winsford, 24 May 1962. (J. Hilton/MLS Collection)

46240 *City of Coventry* waits to depart from Euston with the 9.20pm to Wolverhampton, 4 June 1962.
(MLS Collection)

The final allocation of Duchesses in their last few months was:

Camden:	46246**, 46252**
Crewe North:	46228, 46235, 46239, 46240, 46245, 46248, 46251, 46253**, 46254, 46256 (10)
Edge Hill:	46229, 46233, 46241, 46243
Carlisle Upperby:	46220**, 46221**, 46225, 46234**, 46237, 46238, 46250 (7)
Carlisle Kingmoor:	46226, 46236, 46244, 46247**, 46255, 46257 (6)
Polmadie:	46222**, 46223**, 46224**, 46227*, 46230**, 46231*, 46232*, 46242**, 46249** (9)

* withdrawn in 1962
** withdrawn in 1963

Four Duchesses were stored in the open at Camden at the end of 1962 – 46239, 46240, 46246 and 46252 – and when Camden closed in September 1963 its active Duchesses, 46239, 46240 (both meanwhile restored to traffic) and 46245, were allocated to Willesden before moving on to Crewe North, although 46239 spent a month in August 1964 on loan to Holyhead. Polmadie's 46231 and 46232 had been stored for some time and, with 46227, were the first Duchesses to be withdrawn at the end of 1962. Camden's 46246 was withdrawn in January 1963 without returning to traffic and 46234 (with a cracked frame) and 46253 were condemned at the same time. 46252 lingered on to the end of the winter timetable but was not used before withdrawal. Crewe's 8P Standard 71000 had been withdrawn in November 1962, a sign that it was less valued than the Duchesses. 46248 was removed from store in December 1962 and was used to take the empty Royal Train to Euston, while 46220 *Coronation* performed the last leg of the Royal the next day, taking the Queen from the overnight stabling point at Lowton Junction into Liverpool Lime Street. 46248 *City of Leeds* then took the royal party back to Watford Junction in the afternoon, from where they were returned by car to Windsor Castle. 46220 then worked fitted freight turns from Crewe North. Meanwhile four Duchesses – 46229, 46233, 46241 and 46243 – were stored at Liverpool Edge Hill and 46221 and 46237 at Carlisle Kingmoor. Poor Type 4 diesel availability after the severe winter of 1962/3 caused many of the stored steam engines to be required. There was a redistribution of the remaining active Duchesses in March 1963, when three of the Edge Hill engines were returned to traffic with a regular freight turn, the 7pm St Helen's-Glasgow, which one of them would work instead of a 'Black 5'. 46220 and 46221 were withdrawn in April and 46247 and the stored Camden 46252 in May.

The final Duchess turns were on Crewe to Carlisle/Perth trains, although they occasionally infiltrated the Wolverhampton-Euston and North Wales services. Continuing poor diesel availability caused the re-emergence of the Duchesses from time to time. The three Camden/Willesden engines seemed to have been for relief, special and diesel standbys without any diagrammed turns. 46245 *City of London* was kept in sparkling external condition and was used on a couple of railway enthusiast specials. The last regular Duchess turns from London were on the Saturday late morning *Lakes Express* in July and August 1963 and the Saturday 8.5am Euston-Holyhead boat train in the summer of 1964. 46250 was noted on a pigeon special from Lancashire to Wolverhampton in early June and 46229 was recorded taking over from a failed Type 4 diesel at Preston on 15 July on the 9.30am Manchester-Glasgow.

At the end of the summer timetable of 1963, most Duchesses were in store, although several emerged for the extra services – both parcels and relief passenger trains – over the Christmas period. 46248 was noted on the 10.10am Edinburgh-Birmingham and 46237 on the 10.05am Glasgow-Birmingham on 21 December. 46238 worked an Up Stranraer boat train, 46229 *The Ulster Express* and 46245 a twenty coach ECS train during the same period. Nine Duchesses were seen at work in the run-up to Christmas and nearly all the relief passenger services that Christmas were steam hauled. 46245 *City of London* arrived at Euston on the Up *Royal Scot* on 28 December and 46228 was there on a parcels train on the 29th.

On 2 March 1964 the current was switched on north of Nuneaton and most services changed from diesel to electric traction there, although a few steam services south were noted. There were still twelve Duchesses active then on the West Coast Main Line, most based at Crewe and Carlisle – 46225, 46228, 46235, 46238-46240, 46245, 46248, 46250, 46251, 46254 and 46256. On 13 March, 46254, working the Dagenham-Halewood car components train (a turn often worked by a pacific), ran out of coal that the fireman could easily reach – crews were banned from going into the tender under the wires – so an electric was attached and hauled the train and 46254 to Crewe. Ten days later it appeared at the head of the 7.35am commuter train from Bletchley to Euston. Several Duchesses, 46228, 46239, 46240 and 46251, were used on Grand National specials to Aintree.

Thirteen Duchesses were active over the Easter period. Crewe North's 46228 *Duchess of Rutland* hauled the 320 ton 1pm relief to the *Midday Scot* from Crewe to Carlisle, with speeds over 70mph at Hartford (before a series of signal checks), Leyland, Bay Horse, Hest Bank (78), Tebay (76) and finally 83mph at Eden Valley Junction and 89 at Plumpton. The relief had been hauled by Britannia 70054 to Crewe and arrival at Carlisle was nearly two minutes early in 141 minutes net for the 141.1 miles – actual 154 minutes 45 seconds. Four were seen working relief trains towards London. 46251 worked the 9.50am Crewe-Holyhead on 7 April and was the power for a Nottingham-Swindon RCTS train in May, being photographed at Swindon alongside 7022 *Hereford Castle* which was a standby for the 'Castle' high speed runs of 9 May. However, most of the relief trains for the Whitsun bank holiday were hauled by 'Black 5s' rather than pacifics.

The 1964 summer timetable gave the remaining Duchesses their last opportunities. 46251 worked the 9.30am Manchester-

Cardiff to Shrewsbury on 13 June. 46241 hauled the 10.53 Workington-Euston on Saturday 20 June. 46240 *City of Coventry* had the 395 ton 5.35pm Euston - Holyhead relief on 24 July 1964 and reached Crewe in 166½ minutes (150 net). Signal checks spoiled the climb to Tring but 82mph was touched at Castlethorpe, 61 minimum at Roade, 81 at Weedon (78 minutes net to passing Rugby), and after a 20mph p-way check before Nuneaton, 84 at Hademore and sustained 77-79mph from Rugeley to Milford. Two weeks later on 8 August in its last month before withdrawal, 46228 left Holyhead 17½ minutes late on the 3.30pm relief boat train – 11 coaches, 350 tons gross – and had recovered ten minutes before being forced to stop at Bletchley to take water as there was no water in the Castlethorpe troughs. The time gained was therefore all lost again but the last 46.7 miles were covered in 45 minutes 50 seconds against the easy 63 minute pass-stop schedule so arrival was right on time. 46228 was in a filthy external state by this time, but went well enough with 58 minimum at Tring, and 80 at King's Langley and Wembley.

46239 *City of Chester* worked the regular 8.5 am Euston-Holyhead boat train (11 coaches, 375 tons gross) on the morning of 28 August 1964 and ran the 82 miles to Rugby in 104 minutes arriving a minute early (the times were drastically slowed to allow recovery from the extensive electrification work). The onwards 51 miles from Rugby to Stafford took 54 minutes 51 seconds (49 minutes net) before having to stop there for water, as again the water troughs were out of action – this time at Hademore. 83mph was reached after Tamworth and 82 at Rugeley. Stafford-Crewe was run in 25½ minutes, with 74 minimum at Whitmore and 84 at Betley Road.

North of the Border, Duchesses still regularly worked the 9.25am Crewe-Perth and the 5.30pm Glasgow-Carlisle via Kilmarnock, and the remaining Duchesses were out in force between Crewe and Carlisle on several summer weekends. On the weekend of 23-25 July eight were observed passing Shap and the following weekend there were no fewer than seventeen observations of them over three days.

From 1 September 1964, all Duchesses, Royal Scots, Patriots and Jubilees were banned south of Crewe, any steam-hauled reliefs being allocated to 'Britannias' or 'Black 5s' only. The last run of the *Caledonian* on 4 September 1964 was worked by 46238 *City of Carlisle* from Crewe to Carlisle before withdrawal – surely a special arrangement. On 1 September 46243 was seen on the 11.30am Birmingham-Edinburgh, returning on the 10.10am Edinburgh next day. In the last two weeks, 46250 was seen working from Carlisle to Glasgow, 46239 from Euston to Crewe despite the ban, 46240 on a freight, 46256 from Crewe to Euston also breaking the ban. On 11 September 46228 was seen north of Crewe on a relief, and the next day 46238, 46245 and 46251 were seen at Tebay – the last workings apart from 46256 *Sir William A. Stanier FRS* which was held back for an RCTS tour on 26 September between Crewe and Carlisle in both directions, after which it was condemned on 3 October.

There had been a serious proposal to send twenty of the remaining Duchesses to the Southern Region to replace the remaining Bulleid pacifics on the Waterloo-Bournemouth services, but the extreme curvature through Northam Tunnel just the London side of Southampton Central station was too big an obstacle. The lack of water troughs on the Southern Region would have required an exchange of tender – possibly to a WD 5,000 gallon one as used by 46236 during the 1948 locomotive exchanges.

The earlier withdrawals and those from Camden were broken up at Crewe Works – 46220-46224, 46227, 46230-46232, 46234, 46236, 46242, 46246, 46247, 46249, 46252, 46253. The locomotives that finished at Kingmoor – 46226, 46237, 46238, 46244, 46250, 46255, 46257 – were sold for scrap to Arnott Young based at Troon Harbour. The Duchesses withdrawn from Crewe North were disposed of to Cashmore's of Tipton Staffordshire – 46228, 46239-46241, 46245, 46248, 46251, 46254, 46256. Just one, Edge Hill's 46243, went to the Central Wagon Company at Ince, Wigan, for breaking up.

The Duchesses were missed. Diesel availability continued to be poor and the Britannias struggled with the previous Duchess turns and holiday reliefs and many steam substitutions were double-headed, most frequently by pairs of 'Black 5s'.

The Final Years, 1960–1964 • 57

46220 *Coronation* on arrival at Liverpool Lime Street after working the Royal Train from its overnight stabling point at Lowton Junction, December 1962. (MLS Collection)

Below left: **46252** *City of Leicester* undergoing its routine valves and pistons examination at Longsight depot, 8 July 1962. (MLS Collection)

Below right: **46245** *City of London* leaving Doncaster with the 'Home Counties Railway Society' special to King's Cross, 9 August 1963. (E. Oldham/MLS Collection)

46245 *City of London* as displayed at the Willesden exhibition, 6 October 1963. Preserved LNER B12/3 61572 is in the background. (N. Fields/ MLS Collection)

46225 *Duchess of Gloucester* at Bangor with the 2.45pm Holyhead-Crewe train, c1963. 44865 heads a Down stopping train. (Transport Treasury/ MLS Collection)

The Final Years, 1960–1964 • 59

46236 *City of Bradford* pauses at Gleneagles with the Perth portion of the 10am from Euston, 3 August 1963. (N. Fields/MLS Collection)

46237 *City of Bristol* at the south end of Crewe station on a four-coach local for Shrewsbury alongside new electric E3076 (later a class 85), 12 March 1963. (G. Neve/MLS Collection)

46238 *City* of *Carlisle* gets away from Penrith with the Keswick and Workington portion of the *Lakes Express*, July 1964. (MLS Collection)

46250 *City* of *Lichfield* departs from Oxenholme with the Penrith & Workington portion of the *Lakes Express*, 31 August 1963. (A.C. Gilbert/MLS Collection)

The Final Years, 1960–1964 • 61

Above left: **46239** *City of Chester* at Euston station awaiting arrival of the newspaper vans before departing with the main West Coast newspaper train, June 1963. (D. Loveday/MLS Collection)

Above right: **46240** *City of Coventry* rounds the curve into Stafford station with a Down express, c1964. 46240 has acquired the yellow stripe on the cab side. (Bill Gwyther/MLS Collections)

46250 *City of Lichfield* with a Up express between Bletchley and Tring, c1963. (MLS Collection)

Kingmoor's 46255 *City of Hereford* climbing Beattock Bank at Greskine Box on the Perth portion of the 10am Euston, 27 July 1963. (A.C. Gilbert/MLS Collection)

46248 *City of Leeds* saunters through Hest Bank with the 4pm Glasgow-London milk train, c1963. (D. Cash/MLS Collection)

The Final Years, 1960–1964 • 63

Above left: **Polmadie's 46221** *Queen Elizabeth* and another Duchess at Crewe South depot after the closure of Crewe North, 1963. (MLS Collection)

Above right: **46239** *City of Chester* backing onto a train at Crewe station, 1964. (Bill Gwyther/MLS Collections)

Below: **46251** *City of Nottingham* departing from Chester with the 2.45pm Holyhead-Crewe, 30 June 1964. (J.W. Sutherland/MLS Collection)

46228 Duchess of Rutland on a Down parcels train at Standish Junction, 23 May 1964. (MLS Collection)

46238 City of Carlisle at Skew Bridge with a parcels train, June 1964. (Photomatic/MLS Collection)

The Final Years, 1960–1964 • 65

46238 *City of Carlisle* at Bangor with a Crewe-Holyhead train, 10 August 1964. (MLS Collection)

46240 *City of Coventry* ambles through Nuneaton station with a Down fitted freight train, 1964. (MLS Collection)

66 • THE LMS PRINCESS CORONATION PACIFICS, THE FINAL YEARS & PRESERVATION

46237 *City of Bristol* at Beattock summit with an Easter relief train for Glasgow, 27 March 1964. (MLS Collection)

46256 *Sir William A Stanier* at Golborne on a Down parcels train, 3 May 1964. (R.S. Greenwood/MLS Collection)

Above left: **46254** *City of Stoke-on-Trent* on an Up fitted freight at Carnforth, 11 July 1964. (Harold D. Bowtell/MLS Collection)

Above right: **A rear** view of maroon 46225 *Duchess of Gloucester* standing at Warrington with an Up freight, 21 May 1964. (W.D. Brown/MLS Collection)

Below: **46245** *City of London* with a part fitted freight at Shap Quarry, 20 August 1964. (N. Fields/MLS Collection)

46238 *City of Carlisle* on a Down goods train at Shap Quarry, 20 August 1964. (MLS Collection)

46238 *City of Carlisle* at Oxenholme with the 10.30am Euston-Carlisle semi-fast train, 8 August 1964. (A.C. Gilbert/ MLS Collection)

The Final Years, 1960–1964 • 69

46237 *City of Bristol* with a Carlisle-Birmingham train at Skew Bridge, 8 August 1964. (MLS Collection)

46228 *Duchess of Rutland* at Llandudno Junction with a heavy parcels train, 18 August 1964. (MLS Collection)

70 • THE LMS PRINCESS CORONATION PACIFICS, THE FINAL YEARS & PRESERVATION

A close up of 46228 at Llandudno Junction, showing the deplorable state into which many of the Duchesses had deteriorated a few days before withdrawal, 18 August 1964.
(MLS Collection)

46248 *City of Leeds* at Leyland with an Up express, 29 August 1964.
(R. Farrell/MLS Collection)

The Final Years, 1960–1964 • 71

46243 *City of Lancaster* at St Helen's en route to its final graveyard at Ince Wagon Works where it would be dismantled, August 1964.
(MLS Collection)

Carlisle Upperby's 46225 *Duchess of Gloucester* eases into Preston station with a Christmas parcels special consisting of two vanfits and a brakevan, December 1963.
(MLS Collection)

46251 *City of Nottingham* at Grayrigg with a Stephenson Locomotive Society special from Crewe to Carlisle, 12 July 1964. (H.D. Bowtell/MLS Collection)

46245 *City of London* prepares to leave Crewe South depot to head the Ian Allan railtour for Euston, 1 September 1964. (MLS Collection)

The Final Years, 1960–1964 • 73

46255 *City of Hereford* on a Stephenson Locomotive Society special at Ais Gill, July 1964. (Photomatic/MLS Collection)

46256 *Sir William A. Stanier FRS* at Carlisle after working the last Duchess RCTS railtour before its withdrawal, 26 September 1964. (MLS Collection)

74 • THE LMS PRINCESS CORONATION PACIFICS, THE FINAL YEARS & PRESERVATION

46256 on arrival back at Crewe with the RCTS special from Carlisle, 26 September 1964. 46256 was the sole remaining Stanier pacific in BR operation on this date and was withdrawn a week later. (MLS Collection)

Below left and below right: **Two views** of 46256 *Sir William A. Stanier FRS* with the yellow stripe across the cabside to denote that it is prohibited south of Crewe after electrification. It is seen at Crewe South Depot, 27 September 1964, a day after the withdrawal of the remaining Stanier pacifics. 46256 had been retained for a special working. (MLS Collection)

The Final Years, 1960–1964 • 75

46257 *City of Salford*, 46244 *King George VI*, and 46200 *The Princess Royal* in store at Carlisle Upperby, nameplates removed, 26 February 1964. 46200 had been withdrawn many months before. (Arnold Battson & MLS Collections)

46244 stripped of its *King George VI* nameplates after withdrawal in a row of other condemned Duchesses at Carlisle Upperby shed, 4 October 1964. (MLS Collection)

76 • THE LMS PRINCESS CORONATION PACIFICS, THE FINAL YEARS & PRESERVATION

A line of condemned Duchesses behind the shed at Carlisle Upperby, including from the front 46226, 46225, 46238 and on the far line, 46250, 4 October 1964. (MLS Collection)

46243 formerly named *City of Lancaster* with two 'Jubilees', an 8F and WD 2-8-0 awaiting breaking up at Ince Central Wagon Works, 29 May 1965. (R. Farrell/MLS Collection)

Chapter 4
PERSONAL EXPERIENCE

I described my 1950-56 experiences with Duchess pacifics, small in number, in my first 'Princess Coronation' book. Most of my encounters happened after 1957, by which time I had access to cheap 'privilege' tickets available to serving railwaymen. Therefore, on 10 June 1957 I made my own way to Crewe for a day's spotting, joining the 10.10 Euston-Perth whose 15-coach train was double-headed by 46237 *City of Bristol* and rebuilt Patriot 45540 *Sir Robert Turnbull*. I've no idea whether the provision of the pilot was because of the load, or the need to return the Longsight Patriot to the north. As far as I can remember the train was punctual – with that excess of power it had no excuse to be otherwise – and after a good day at the railway enthusiasts' 'mecca', I was about to return home with the *Midday Scot* for which a gleaming Camden Duchess (46229 *Duchess of Hamilton*) was poised, when the Liverpool-London *Red Rose* glided into the station behind 46205 *Princess Victoria* and I was tempted by that – and experienced a fine run with speeds after Tring in the high eighties.

46229 *Duchess of Hamilton* stands at Crewe ready to take over the Up *Midday Scot*, April 1957. (David Maidment)

I spent a week's holiday in August 1957 on the Clyde coast at Dunoon with a group of students and of course chose to go north on the Saturday *Royal Scot* booked non-stop in the public timetable, but just a working stop near Kingmoor depot to change crews. I was looking forward to a Polmadie Duchess, my mind harking back to my 1950/1 experience, but it was Camden's 46244 *King George VI* that backed down. I can see it in my mind's eye now, a lovely blue, except it wasn't. My mind is playing tricks as by 1957 46244 was the standard BR green. I can only assume that my brain is jumping to an earlier trainspotting trip to view the *Royal Scot* after the diagram had changed to a Camden engine and 46244 had paraded then in blue. I did take a few speed readings from the rail joints on the climb to Shap and can recall that we climbed steadily from Scout Green at around 30mph with our maximum load of around 13-14 coaches. I returned a week later on the *Midday Scot* but got two Princess Royal pacifics – 46203 to Crewe and 46209 to Euston.

The next three years were spent at London University using Southern Region services to commute from Woking with Western Region experience at Old Oak Common during the vacations. The next opportunity I had to experience runs behind Stanier pacifics was not until I had joined the railway as a permanent employee. I celebrated my entitlement to 'quarter-rate privilege' tickets at the very first opportunity, with evening trips to Peterborough and Swindon, which offered various options for steam haulage, unlike the evening services to Rugby by that time, which were all booked for EE type 4 diesels.

However, in early September 1961 I took a day off to time the non-stop weekday *Elizabethan* from King's Cross to Edinburgh with 60009 *Union of South Africa*. I crossed to Glasgow behind an A3, took a trip out from St Enoch to Kilmarnock with a Corkerhill 'Jubilee' and finished up at the Central station in time to get the 8.55pm Fridays Only to Euston which on that date, 1 September, was worked by Polmadie's 46232 *Duchess of Montrose*. The load was 12 coaches 424/445 tons and the whole run was conducted in a spectacular thunderstorm. We left Motherwell five minutes late after a p-way slowing from Newton to Uddingston and suffered three more at Law Junction, Braidwood and Beattock station. We took 114½ minutes from Motherwell to Carlisle (net 102 minutes) for the 89½ miles with curiously uneven running. After climbing to Beattock summit at a minimum of 41mph we descended very cautiously, braking to 60mph as soon as speed approached 70, and just touched 73 before slowing for the Beattock station slack. A final 77mph at Gretna Green looked likely to enable a punctual arrival at Carlisle but a severe signal check at Floriston put paid to that and we arrived three minutes late. I got the impression that the driver was unused to driving such a large engine as he seemed nervous of really opening it out and kept touching the brake when speed was getting towards the seventies except for the final rush to reach Carlisle on time. I'd intended to watch the night working at Carlisle (always a fascinating experience at that time) before picking up a St Pancras-Edinburgh train via the Waverley route in the early morning, though I admit I was severely tempted to change plans when 46232 cut off at Carlisle and was replaced by 46206 *Princess Marie Louise*. I reluctantly stuck to my plan and got a Peak (D11) to Hawick where I baled out for a B1 on a stopper and returned to London on the 10.10 SO relief to the *Heart of Midlothian*, with an A3, A1 and another A3 – luckily all splendid runs.

Whilst weekday evenings were unpromising for steam haulage out of Euston, Saturday operations gave some opportunity, even if it was a question of waiting to seize the chance. I had a free Friday in April 1962 just before three months training at Old Oak Common in possession of a Western Region footplate pass, and hung around Euston to see if I could catch a Duchess or Scot. I was in luck, for the 10.25am to Windermere produced Upperby's 46225 *Duchess of Gloucester*. Our 450-ton train was banked to Camden by 75031, but the Duchess primed and we didn't really get going before suffering a 10mph p-way slowing at Bushey. We had only recovered to 54mph by Apsley and had already fallen to 51 at Hemel Hempstead before another p-way slowing to 30mph at Berkhamsted. A signal check to 15mph at Bletchley, and more p-way severe checks at both Weedon and Welton and a final stand outside Rugby completed a pretty miserable run in 112¼ minutes. I tried again on the following day, 3 April, when 46225 again backed down onto the 1.5pm to Perth. We did much better this time, getting our 455 ton train to Rugby in 100 minutes (83 net) with 58mph minimum at Tring, 76 at Leighton Buzzard, 74 at Castlethorpe, 63 minimum at Roade and 75 at Weedon before a final string of checks – p-way and signals – delayed our arrival. This was a time of course when electrification work was in full swing and schedules were much extended to take account of the frequent slowings required. I returned from Rugby with 46170 on a featherweight semi-fast train on the Friday and an overloaded rebuilt Patriot (45527) on the Saturday.

I decided to try again three weeks later on 23 April and took 46136 on a very pedestrian semi-fast train via Northampton. Although it was going to Crewe, I decided to await something better from Rugby, anticipating a Duchess on the Perth. It was 46225 again, so I mistakenly let it go awaiting something different and in the end had to satisfy myself with a Type 40 diesel. At least at Crewe I found the 4.40pm Liverpool-Euston relief arriving with 46228 *Duchess of Rutland* and climbed aboard eagerly. The load was 15 coaches, 472/505 tons and after a p-way slack to 18mph at Betley Road we accelerated to 55mph at Whitmore summit and touched 70 (just) before the Stafford stop. A prolonged check in the Colwich area caused by sheep on the line was followed by running in the low 70s before the Nuneaton stop. Then more signal checks made us late into Rugby. 74 by Weedon was good as was 63 at Roade and 76 at Castlethorpe before more delays between Wolverton and Bletchley. 61 at Tring was followed by 78 at Hemel Hempstead and then a crawl caused by signal checks all the way from King's Langley to Bushey followed by a 12 minute stand on the bank outside Euston awaiting a platform made us 20 minutes late despite the easy schedule.

In June 1963 I discovered the Glasgow-Aberdeen 3-hour trains booked for Gresley A3s and A4s and spent a few days each summer between then and 1966 savouring many splendid runs. In between the A4s I came across 46244 *King George VI* at Perth heading the 8.15pm to Kensington Olympia, which managed to accelerate its 8-coach 275 ton train from a 10mph p-way check at the foot of the 1 in 100 to 37mph through Auchterarder before the Gleneagles stop. Three extra coaches were added at Stirling and I decanted at Larbert as I had a further day planned in Scotland. I therefore found myself at Glasgow Central the following evening, Friday 21 June, and opted to return to London on the 8.55pm FO Glasgow-Euston that I'd seen Duchess and Princess Royal hauled in the autumn of 1961. I was in luck, it was still steam and Kingmoor's 46244 turned up again to take us to Carlisle. The load was lighter this time, 10 coaches, 309/325 tons. 46244 took it pretty easily, and after Motherwell, with 70 at Lamington, topped Beattock at 51mph, coasting down the other side and with nothing over 68mph thereafter arrived in Carlisle a couple of minutes early. 46244 was replaced by an Upperby Duchess, 46238 *City of Carlisle,* and I kept

46244 *King* George VI at Perth with the 8.15pm for Kensington Olympia, 20 June 1963. Schoolboy spotters are seen 'cabbing' the pacific.
(David Maidment)

awake long enough to time it to Preston (passing there at 1.15am). Being a night train, the schedule was easy, and we took 43½ minutes to clear Shap summit at 38mph with nothing over 68 at Tebay. We reached 70 at Milnthorpe and 71 at Garstang between p-way checks. I slept until Rugby passed at 4.8am and we continued at a steady 60-68 mph until a string of severe checks between Castlethorpe and Tring, the cause of which was discovered to be a derailment on the main line at Cheddington. There followed electrification p-way checks at Apsley, Watford, Willesden Junction and Queens Park and a signal stand on Camden bank, making us 12 minutes late on arrival.

I was getting disappointed with none of my Duchess runs matching the A3s and A4s (admittedly with much lighter loads) on both the East Coast south of Grantham and in Scotland. However, the tide was about to turn. In the summer of 1963, the 11.40am Euston-Windermere *Lakes Express* was a regular Duchess turn and I managed three runs as far as its first stop at Wigan, carrying on to Preston on two of them. The first was an excellent run, the driver pushing 46254 hard between innumerable checks (some caused by early running) only spoilt by a series of signal stands at Warrington making our arrival in Wigan nearly 14 minutes late after running ahead of schedule until then. My log of this run is below:

Euston-Wigan

46254 *City of Stoke-on-Trent* **5A**

11.40am Euston - Windermere

12 chs, 413/430 tons

6.7.1963

Miles	Location	Times	Speeds	Punctuality	Gradients
0	Euston	00.00		¾ L	Banker 44839
1.1	Camden No.1	03.42	23		1/70 R. 1/112 R
	Queen's Park	09.02	pws 25*/42		
5.4	Willesden Junction	11.58	pws 26*	3¾ L	
8.3	Wembley Central	16.44	52½		1/339 R
11.4	Harrow & Wealdstone	20.36	61/pws 50*		1/339 R
15.9	Bushey	25.30	59/65		
17.4	Watford	26.53	68		1/708 F, 1/393 R
20.9	King's Langley	30.09	66		
	Apsley	35.26	pws 3*		
24.5	Hemel Hempstead	37.53	46/53		1/335 R
28	Berkhamsted	42.00	62		1/335 R
31.7	Tring	45.51	68/70		1/335 R, L
36.1	Cheddington	50.55	77/ pws 10*		1/333 F
40.2	Leighton Buzzard	56.15	63/74		
46.7	Bletchley	61.59	80/pws 32*		L
	Denbigh Hall Sdgs	-	pws 28*		
	Milton Keynes	-	64		

		Euston-Wigan			
		46254 *City of Stoke-on-Trent* 5A			
		11.40am Euston - Windermere			
		12 chs, 413/430 tons			
		6.7.1963			
Miles	Location	Times	Speeds	Punctuality	Gradients
52.4	Wolverton	70.01	74		1/440 F, L
54.8	Castlethorpe	72.02	75		
59.9	Roade	76.37	67½		1/330 R
62.8	Blisworth	-	80/83		1/320 F
69.7	Weedon	-	82		L
75.3	Welton	89.18	72/70		1/350 R
	Hillmorton Box	93.40	77/sigs 5*		1/370 F
		96.29/96.48	sigs stand		
82.6	Rugby	101.00	pws 5*	¼ E	
88.1	Brinklow	109.19	65		L
	Shilton	112.20	69		1/330 R
93.4	Bulkington	-	75		L
97.1	Nuneaton	117.17	82	T	1/320 F
102.3	Atherstone	121.25	76/84		
106.5	Polesworth	124.40	85		1/321 F
110	Tamworth	127.20	81/70*		
	Hademore	130.28	73/66½		1/376 R
116.3	Lichfield	133.00	62	3 E	1/331 R
121	Armitage	138.05	65		
124.3	Rugeley	141.09	62/65	3 E	
127.2	Colwich	144.05	72		
		147.02/147.45 sigs stand			
	Milford	149.25	pws 20*		
133.6	Stafford	158.02	48	3 L	
138.9	Norton Bridge	163.54	68		1/517 R
143.4	Standon Bridge	-	72		1/650 R
147.6	Whitmore	172.15	68		1/398 R
150.1	Madeley	174.28	74/83	¼ E	1/348 F
153.3	Betley Road	176.53	87		1/177 F
	Basford Hall	179.54	sigs 36*		

		Euston-Wigan			
		46254 *City of Stoke-on-Trent* 5A			
		11.40am Euston - Windermere			
		12 chs, 413/430 tons			
		6.7.1963			
Miles	Location	Times	Speeds	Punctuality	Gradients
	Crewe South	182.15/185.10 sigs stand		6 E	
158.1	Crewe	188.52/189.58 sigs stand		¾ L	
	Coppenhall Junction	196.20	58		L
166.9	Winsford	200.20	76	3 E	1/300 F
169.9	Hartford	204.24	82/sigs 18*		
174.3	Weaver Junction	211.04	67		
	Norton Crossing	-	pws 30*		
180.4	Acton Grange Jn	218.08	54		1/135 R
		220.45/220.58 sigs stand		2½ E	
182.2	Warrington	223.50/229.25 sigs stand			
		230.53/231.28 sigs stand		8½ L	
	Dallam Branch Sdgs	-	sigs 10*		
	Winwick Junction	238.12	52		
	Golborne Junction	241.00	56½		1/132 R, 1/156 R
	Golborne	242.11	61/72		1/473 R, 1/417 F
	Bamfurlong Junction	-	74		L
	Wigan South	-	sigs 5*/ 1*		
193.9	Wigan	250.50	(195 net)	13¾ L	

My estimation of the net time is probably on the conservative side, and it was possibly a mile-a-minute run. The acceleration from each slack was very vigorous and rapid with a beautiful clear cut steady exhaust. My expectations had been raised by that run and I tried it again three weeks later when 46229 *Duchess of Hamilton*, then shedded at Edge Hill, backed on to 13 very full coaches, 428/470 tons. We were banked out of Euston by Ivatt 4MT 43052 and ran steadily just reaching 60mph by Watford before the first p-way slack at Apsley. Progress was more sedate than that of 46254, though less interrupted and we cleared Tring at 59mph and then cantered along at 70-76mph all the way to Castlethorpe, dropping to 60 at Roade. Despite a couple more p-way slacks, we passed Rugby nearly 2 minutes early but then stopped at Nuneaton for water, presumably having failed to pick up sufficient at the troughs shortly after Rugby. I thought the sparks might now fly as we left Nuneaton 11 minutes late but after 77 at Polesworth speed ranged between 60 and 72 all the way to Crewe, where, with the help of 6 minutes recovery time, we threaded the station at 30mph 4 minutes late. Warrington was passed on time despite a diversion to the slow line through the station and we arrived and left Wigan 1½ minutes late. We climbed the 1 in 104 to Boars Head at 42mph and, with 70 at Euxton Junction, were 2 minutes early into Preston. Although the locomotive working was less spectacular than that of 46254, one might surmise that it was a more efficient run, not wasting steam by early running and thereby sustaining fewer signal checks.

On 24 August, 46238 *City of Carlisle* was in charge of the 12 coach 414/450 ton train. After a slow start, falling to 14mph on the climb to Camden even though banked by a Fairburn 2-6-4T, the pacific gradually accelerated to 65mph by Watford and after the severe p-way slack at Apsley, cleared Tring at 52mph. The descent could tempt no more than 72 from our driver, and after a 45mph check through Milton Keynes, recovered to 68 at Castlethorpe, 60 minimum at Roade and 74 at Blisworth before p-way slacks both sides of Weedon. We arrived at Rugby on time but the Stanier pacifics seem thirsty beasts and we stood for nine minutes taking water there (perhaps the troughs between Rugby and Brinklow were still out of order). 75mph was achieved by Nuneaton but running then became very 'ordinary' with no speed higher than 70mph all the way to Crewe and little time recovered until the 'spare' 6 minutes approaching the latter passed slowly 2 minutes late. Performance then deteriorated with signal checks at Hartford and Acton Grange and another p-way slack at Norton Crossing, culminating in a dead stand outside Warrington and a further nine minute delay while 46238 took water again at Warrington platform. Wigan was reached 16 minutes late, but smart work there saved a couple of minutes and arrival at Preston was 10 minutes late.

Earlier that month I had what I can only describe as a spectacular run though not necessarily the most meritorious. I found a curious 3.48pm Crewe-Glasgow (Tues, Thurs & Fri Only) in the timetable and decided it was a good bet for a steam turn. I duly found six coaches (187 tons) waiting forlornly in a bay platform at the north end of Crewe station, and 3.48 came and went with no sign of any passengers or engine. I was just assuming I had misread the timetable when, instead of the expected Black 5, pacific 46235 *City of Birmingham* suddenly appeared and was hastily coupled up. We finally left at five minutes past four, over 17 minutes late, and after a crawl out past Coppenhall Junction at 10mph over a p-way slack, our driver let rip and 46235 accelerated to 75mph like a jet going down the runway. We slowed to 62 at Acton Bridge, then swooped to 80 at Norton Crossing, stopping at Warrington in 28¾ minutes. We were on the receiving end of a number of signal checks at Winwick Junction, Springs Branch (a dead stand), Preston (another dead stand), Garstang, Lancaster, although in between 46235 had roared up to 75 at Euxton Junction, 74 at Barton and 75 at Oubeck between the checks. With a much clearer road from Lancaster the run now moved up another plane and I show below the log from Lancaster onwards:

46229 *Duchess of Hamilton*, now based at Edge Hill, Liverpool, at the head of the 11.40am Euston *Lakes Express* to Windermere, 27 July 1963. (David Maidment)

Lancaster-Carlisle

46235 *City of Birmingham* 5A

6 chs 187/200 tons

3.48pm Crewe (TTHF O) – Glasgow

1.8.1963

Miles	Location	Times	Speeds		Gradients
0	Warrington	00.00		20 L	
47.9	Lancaster	70.10	pws 20 *	35 L	
51	Hest Bank	74.55	70/75		L
54.2	Carnforth	77.25	84/81		
	Burton & Holme	81.35	75½ / sigs 40*		1/134 R
61.5	Milnthorpe	84.14	67		L, 1/173 R
63.4	Hincaster Junction	86.07	71		1/193 R, 1/392 R
67	Oxenholme	89.23	68		1/111 R
	Lambrigg Crossing	-	62		1/131 R
74.1	Grayrigg	96.30	59		1/106 R
75.8	Low Gill	98.13	76		
	Dillicar	-	79		L
80.1	Tebay	101.13	89		L, 1/146 R
83.1	Scout Green	103.44	67		1/75 R
85.6	Shap summit	106.30	62/sigs 50*/ 54		1/75 R
	Shap	108.25	73		1/142 F
	Thrimby Grange	-	78/81		1/125 F
94.9	Clifton & Lowther	114.17	83		1/125 F
	Eden Valley Junction	-	85		1/125 F
99.2	Penrith	118.43	pws 15*		
	Plumpton	123.25	82		1/186 F
106.2	Calthwaite	-	87/94		L, 1/172 F
	Southwaite	127.30	78		1/228 F
112.1	Wreay	-	pws 25*		
<u>117</u>	<u>Carlisle Citadel</u>	<u>136.15</u>		<u>1¼ L</u>	

I subsequently found out the reason for such haste. The turn was unbalanced and the crew had a two minute connection at Carlisle for the next southbound service, otherwise they had a two-hour wait. The crew were jumping out of the cab almost before the train stopped and rushing across the tracks to the London express already standing in the main Up platform! It is almost impossible to calculate the net time from Crewe, but it is around 58 minutes for the 67.1 miles from Lancaster. 94mph

Personal Experience • 85

46235 *City of Birmingham* passing through Stirling with an Aberdeen-London fish train, August 1963. (David Maidment])

was the highest speed I personally experienced behind a Duchess. The descent through Calthwaite was thrilling. I was in the first coach and great lumps of coal were flying off the tender as we hurtled down past the former Calthwaite station. We changed engines at Carlisle – a relief crew removed 46235 and a Standard 5, 73121, took over for a much less dramatic ride to Glasgow. I then spent a couple of days on the Glasgow-Aberdeen line before returning home on an overnight train that produced 46235 once more right through from Carlisle to Euston. I regret I was exhausted and slept fitfully most of the way.

The following summer I went north from my work in South Wales connecting with the 9.25 Crewe-

The new order – an ex-works unnamed 'Britannia' meets a Duchess at Crewe North in its last summer of 1964, a Standard pacific which will seek to cover the remaining needed steam passenger turns until electrification and dieselisation is completed in the North West. (MLS Collection)

Perth, which was booked for a Kingmoor Stanier pacific north of Carlisle the previous two summers, but this time was 70007 *Coeur-de-Lion*, one of the Britannias come to replace them. The summer of 1964 was the last one for the Princess Coronation pacifics and 70007 would be the first Britannia to be withdrawn less than a year later and others would soon be stored. After two days of A4s, an A2 and V2s, for my return I aimed for the 11.45pm FO Edinburgh-Birmingham that I thought was the best chance of steam and felt fortunate to see a Stanier pacific backing down to replace the Black 5 in the darkness at Carlisle. It was green 46237 *City of Bristol* and we set off, but not all seemed to be well. A lot of sparks were flying past the window illuminating the darkness, and although the load was modest – 10 coaches, 350 tons gross – the 45mph on the 1 in 228 past Southwaite fell away to 37 at Calthwaite, then brakes went on, and we halted for six minutes at Plumpton, the fireman working furiously on the fire. We crawled through Penrith having taken 40 minutes for the initial 18 miles, stopped for the crew to speak to the signalman at Eden Valley Junction and drew into the loop at Clifton & Lowther, 46237 declared a failure. It appeared that 46237 had dropped part of its fire through broken or missing firebars and it cut off and disappeared into the night leaving us stranded for 40 minutes. We were fortunate to find that Upperby sent another Duchess to rescue us, 46250 *City of Lichfield*. Starting out of the loop on the 1 in 125 gradient, 46250 had several bouts of slipping, and after reaching 38mph at Thrimby Grange, slipped back literally to 35 before getting a grip again and holding 37 at the top of the 1 in 142 before Shap station, accelerating to 46 on the short level stretch and clearing the summit at 45. We coasted down past Scout Green, braked at 65mph, then coasted some more reaching 73 at Tebay. A p-way slowing at Grayrigg preceded 72 down through Oxenholme and continuing on in the mid-60s, I lost interest and went to sleep only checking on arrival at Wolverhampton that 46250 was still in charge. I transferred to the low level station for a Saturday Wolverhampton-Ilfracombe heavy holiday train with an Oxley Castle (5063), returning from Bristol back to Birmingham New Street behind a former King's Cross B1 (!) and then concluded a hectic few days with another Britannia (70010) back to Euston. The Britannias, rugged simple two-cylinder engines, were deemed more suited in the declining maintenance situation of the final couple of years for the remaining steam work on the West Coast Main Line.

Nearly twenty years later in March 1983, when I was the London Midland Region's Chief Operating Manager, my senior traction inspector, knowing my interest, hinted that I should satisfy myself on the correct and safe operation of the steam specials we were running at the time, and I was invited to join the ex- LNWR support coach on 1Z38 charter train from Euston to Carlisle at Leeds City. The train was routed via Carnforth and duly arrived behind 'Black 5' 5407 some 15 minutes late and I was met by John Peck, the National Railway Museum's engineer in charge of 46229 *Duchess of Hamilton* which was backing on to the 14-coach 535 ton train, 565 tons gross. At Hellifield I was invited to join Inspector Arthur Morris of Preston, and Skipton Driver Ken Iveson and Fireman John Brown on 46229's footplate. The Duchess was in superb condition and I was treated to an exemplary run, which I hasten to add fully met my professional scrutiny as a well-planned and safe tour. I took notes of the engine's working which I table below:

Hellifield-Garsdale, 1Z38 Charter Train

46229 *Duchess of Hamilton* – National Railway Museum

14 chs, 535½ / 565 tons

12.3.1983

Miles	Location	Times	Speeds	Gradients	Cut-off	Regulator	Steam pressure
0	Hellifield	00.00	13¾ L		45%	Full	250
1.5	Long Preston	02.55	48/55	1/214 F	15%	Eased	

Hellifield-Garsdale, 1Z38 Charter Train

46229 *Duchess of Hamilton* – National Railway Museum

14 chs, 535½ / 565 tons

12.3.1983

Miles	Location	Times	Speeds		Gradients		Working	
3.3	Settle Junction	05.09	60	11¾ L	1/181 F	15%	Full	
5.2	Settle	07.15	54/48		1/100 R	15%	Full	250
	Stainforth	-	42		1/100 R	20%	Full	
	MP 240	-	38		1/100 R	30%	Full	Blowing off
11.2	Horton-in-Ribblesdale	-	38/42		1/100 R	35%	Full	
					(gradient eased to 1/200 for a couple of ¼ mile stretches)			
			46			30%	Full	250
	Selside IBS	19.00	43		1/100 R	30%	Full	
16	Ribblehead	-	45		1/100 R	30%	Full	250
17.3	Blea Moor	26.20	34	6 L	1/100 R	40%	Full	240
	Blea Moor Tunnel	-	slipping		1/100 R, 1/440 F		Eased	
	Dent Head	-	20*		1/264 F	30%	Half	230
22.2	Dent	35.22	45/20*	2 L	1/264 R	30%	¼	225
	Rise Hill Tunnel	-	45	L		30%	¼	
			5* slow searching for watering point					
25.4	<u>Garsdale</u>	<u>42.30</u>		<u>1 L</u>				

Two photographs of 46229 with the author on the footplate approaching Ribblehead Viaduct at 45mph with the 14 coach 505 ton *Cumbrian Mountain Express*, 12 March 1983. Both photos, which appeared in a railway magazine at the time, were presented to the author as a souvenir of his first footplate trip on a Princess Coronation pacific. (Author's Collection)

The fire was deliberately run down from Ribblehead to avoid blowing off steam at the Garsdale watering point. The inspector calculated that 46229 had used 2,000 gallons of water from Leeds, that is 32½ gallons per mile. Apart from the slip entering Blea Moor Tunnel, the engine had been very sure-footed and rode superbly like a Pullman coach, the cab silent from the usual vibrations and rattling experienced on most steam engine footplates.

On 30 September and 2 and 3 October 1995, three special steam trials promoted by the staff of the *Railway Magazine* were held over the Grayrigg and Shap gradients testing the performance of an A4, the BR 8P 'Duke' and the preserved Duchess 46229. The load was the same each day, 11 coaches, for around 430 tons gross. The test section started at Milnthorpe where each was limited to 60mph to ensure an equal start and were restricted to 60 again at Tebay so that it was a test of sheer power rather than rushing the bank. A4 60007 *Sir Nigel Gresley* went first and topped Grayrigg at 40mph, but injector problems forced its driver to ease near the summit. The A4 was opened up on Shap with cut-off at 55 per cent by Scout Green Box and then 67 per cent which caused the A4 to slip and speed drop sharply from the upper 40s to 39mph which then gradually tailed off to 35 at the summit. Maximum recorded power was an edhp of 1,829 at Scout Green just before the slip. The *Duke of Gloucester* was on form and stormed both summits at 61 and 51mph respectively, recording power outputs of 2,366edhp on Grayrigg and a colossal 2,745 on Shap.

A photo from the footplate of 46229 at Hellifield taken by the author as the *Cumbrian Mountain Express* departs for Garsdale and Carlisle. (David Maidment)

The LNWR Brake saloon acting as the NRM support coach in which the author travelled from Leeds to Hellifield and on return from Carlisle as a guest of the National Railway Museum's engineer, John Peck, seen at Hellifield, 12 March 1983. (David Maidment)

46229 *Duchess of Hamilton* on the Cumbrian Mountain Express taking water and cleaning the fire at Garsdale, 12 March 1983. (David Maidment)

46229 was the last to go and there was much excitement to see if it could beat the times and power output of the 'Duke' which had set such a high target. The times and speeds over the test sections for the Duchess were:

Milnthorpe-Shap Summit, 3.10.1995

46229 *Duchess of Hamilton* – NRM

11 chs, 406/443 tons

Driver Frank Santrian, Fireman Bob Morrison, Insp Kevin Treeby

Miles	Location	Times	Speeds	Gradient	Power output (edhp)
0	Milnthorpe	00.00	60		
2	Hincaster Junction	02.05	56/61	1/173 R, 1/392 R	979
5.25	Oxenholme	05.04	69/65	1/111 R, 1/178 R	
8.4	Hay Fell	08.08	63	1/131 R	2,317
11	Lambrigg Crossing	10.33	54	1/106 R	
12.25	Grayrigg	12.08	45	1/106 R	1,729
	Low Gill	-	22	L	
18.5	Tebay	20.17	56½	L, 1/146 R	2,055
22	Scout Green Box	24.14	47	1/75 R	2,523
23.5	Shap Summit	26.58	41½	1/75 R	2,081

There were problems on the footplate. Frank Santrian later reported that they were having injector trouble near the summit of Grayrigg Bank and one safety valve was failing to reseat properly, the pressure dropping to 180lb psi, so they slowed at Low Gill to allow time for the boiler to be pulled round before the assault on Shap. To compensate for the low pressure, Santrian increased to cut-off successively to a full 75 per cent by Scout Green producing 46229's highest power output but this could not be sustained and both power and speed dropped over the last mile. There is no doubt that 71000 took the honours on this occasion, and 46229 was inhibited from equalling that performance by its injector and safety valve problems. The three trial trains returned via the Settle & Carlisle with the trial of strength on the climb from Appleby to Ais Gill. 60007 was not steaming well with a dirty fire and much ash in the smokebox and was fortunate to make a respectable climb with an average edhp of 1,080. 71000 again did well though not producing the same effort as on Shap, with exhaust injector problems causing a slight easing with an average edhp of just 2,000.

46229 with a new crew of Driver John Finlayson and Fireman Brian Grierson with Inspector John McCabe passed Appleby at 55mph, speed rising to 74½ on Ormside Viaduct, and dropping quickly to 54 on the 1 in 100 at Helm Tunnel. It fell to 45 at the top of the initial 1 in 100 at Griseburn, rose to 57½ on the easing of the grades past Crosby Garrett and then fell to 46 on the 1 in 100 at Kirkby Stephen, and 44 at Birkett Tunnel. 46229 accelerated to 52 when the gradient eased to 1 in 330 to Mallerstang and then fell again to 45 at the summit of the 1 in 100 at Ais Gill. 46229 had been beaten by 71000 again – it was not 46229's day, although the performance would have been considered admirable on any other occasion. The maximum power output on this leg was 1,783edhp on the last stretch to Ais Gill, the average for the climb being 1,591edhp. Had 46229 been in the same condition as my footplate run in 1983, I have every confidence that it could have at least equalled if not beaten 71000. Apparently both exhaust and live steam injectors 'knocked off' on the climb and 46229 had to be eased. At the end of the day 46229 achieved one last triumph, outshining the other two locomotives on the 3 mile 1 in 82 of Whalley bank, climbing at 42/38mph, whilst both other competitors seemed 'weary' by then, 71000 climbing at a steady 30mph whilst 60007 was really struggling and fell to 14mph near the top of the bank.

Nearly seven years later, a Duchess in superb condition showed what 46229 should have been capable of. I joined the 6.2am Birmingham International-Carlisle at Crewe, where 46233 *Duchess of Sutherland* replaced the odd pairing of diesels 33 108 and 31 602. The load was exactly the same as the trial runs, 11 coaches, 402/430 tons. We set off on time, 75mph by Hartford and 79 at Moore and despite two p-way slacks at Warrington and Golborne Junction, with another 78 at Balshaw Lane, we made Barton Loop for a water stop on time. A half hour sprint with 78mph at Bay Horse got us inside Carnforth Goods Loop in good time for a Birmingham-Glasgow Voyager to pass and we left 5 minutes early. I will then show the Milnthorpe-Shap Summit timings in the same format as the 46229 trial for comparison.

Milnthorpe-Shap Summit, 20.4.2002

46233 *Duchess of Sutherland*

11 chs, 402/430 tons

Driver Bill Andrew, Fireman Frank Santrian

Miles	Location	Times	Speeds	Gradient
0	Milnthorpe	00.00	64	
2	Hincaster Junction	01.55	61	1/173 R, 1/392 R
5.25	Oxenholme	05.28	57/59	1/111 R, 1/178 R
8.4	Hay Fell	-	55	1/131 R
11	Lambrigg Crossing	-	52	1/106 R
12.25	Grayrigg	13.55	51½ / pws 17*	1/106 R
	Low Gill	18.47	pws/43	L
	Dillicar	-	68	L

Milnthorpe-Shap Summit, 20.4.2002

46233 *Duchess of Sutherland*

11 chs, 402/430 tons

Driver Bill Andrew, Fireman Frank Santrian

Miles	Location	Times	Speeds	Gradient
18.5	Tebay	22.30	78	L, 1/146 R
22	Scout Green Box	-	60½	1/75 R
	MP 37	-	49*/48	1/75 R
23.5	Shap Summit	28.09	53	1/75 R

46233 lost time against 46229 by observing a mile long 15mph permanent way slack from Grayrigg to Low Gill but then accelerated furiously to Tebay starting the main climb at 78 rather than 60. 46233's driver caught sight of a momentary yellow at the Scout Green IBS and shut off losing some 7-8mph, but it cleared to green immediately and 46233 was then opened up and even gradually accelerated to the summit. After another long p-way slack at Thrimby Grange we ran in the upper 70s after Eden Valley Junction with a maximum of 77 at Plumpton and were then kept waiting outside Carlisle station until 60009 had departed for the Settle & Carlisle line some 14 minutes late. Even so we were still a minute early into Carlisle station. We returned via the same route and from a pathing stop in the Goods Loop at Eden Valley Junction accelerated to 47mph at Thrimby Grange, 51 at Shap station and 54 at the summit before easily touching 77mph at Scout Green, Dillicar, Oxenholme and Burton & Holme. We arrived early into Carnforth Goods Loop, left 21 minutes early ahead of late running service trains and followed a Glasgow-Birmingham Voyager 16 minutes early from Preston. Running under light steam at around 70mph after Warrington, we could have been very early into Crewe but were held outside and eventually ran into platform 12 just four minutes early. And that was my last and worthy example of Duchess performance.

I visit the National Railway Museum at York quite frequently and see 46229 in its streamlined guise. I know it looks impressive, but for me I preferred the Duchess in her de-streamlined form – that is how I really knew her.

Chapter 5
RAILWAYMEN REMEMBER

In July 2021 Gordon Heddon, Hon Chairman of the Crewe Heritage Centre, introduced me to three former Crewe North drivers who had been firemen in the heyday of the Duchesses – Les Jackson, Neil Cadman and Bill Andrew – and a Crewe Works fitter, Keith Collier. I persuaded them (with very little reluctance!) to talk about their experiences, interviewing Les Jackson at his home and Neil, Bill and Keith with Gordon Heddon at the Crewe Heritage site. Les, Bill and Keith gave me written records of some of their memories and all four gave me further data and photographs and I will use some of their words now. Both Les and Bill were also drivers of Duchesses in the preservation era on main line charter trains and Keith became the chief mechanical engineer for the restoration of 71000 *Duke of Gloucester* between 1992 and 2012, after working on it in Crewe Works in 1985 and joining its preservation society as a leading fitter. Although I'll refer to the numbers of engines they mentioned with their BR numbers, the drivers always used the old LMS numbering without the BR '4' prefix. The highlight of their careers as firemen when they regularly were assigned to the Duchess pacifics was in Link 2, the Crewe-Perth link. This consisted of eight sets of men who worked round the turns in an eight week cycle. Two strenuous weeks consisted of three return overnight Crewe-Perth turns, 296 miles each way, lodging in Perth during the intervening day. Five more weeks required two return night runs. The final week included London and Glasgow trips on the *Midday Scot* to retain the men's route knowledge. Link 3 to which these drivers refer was the Glasgow link, again mainly overnight work on the sleepers, mail and newspaper trains. Many Crewe men avoided the Perth link because of its almost continuous night work and lodging turns, others loved it and moved quickly to that link ahead of others who preferred the day London turns in Link 1.

Les Jackson

Les frequented (and often operated) a signal box at his home in Workington as a boy and became a cleaner at Workington shed in 1952. After National Service in Germany, he moved to Bletchley and in February 1957 as a fireman to Crewe North where he was placed in a link known as the 'Block' – 200 sets of men that covered everything of a general nature rostered to the depot. His first trip to Glasgow was on 'Black 5' 45300 coupled to another with 17 coaches – they had to drop 44766 off en route at Polmadie to avoid blocking the throat to Glasgow Central station with the tail of their train. His first Duchess was with 46254 running in after a Works repair on a three-coach Crewe-Manchester stopping train, where he discovered the limited brake power of the three coaches to stop 150 tons of engine as well as 100 tons of coaches.

In 1961 he was promoted to the Glasgow link and remembered firing the *Midday Scot* from Crewe to Glasgow on his favourite Duchess, 46248 *City of Leeds* (which for many years was Crewe North's royal engine), and after a perfect trip north returned on 46220 *Coronation*, staggering up to Beattock with 16 on, pistons blowing, and then haring down the other side 'rocking and rolling', the speedometer showing 100mph. Apparently, after expressing some concern to his driver, he got the response ' if we roll over you won't feel a bloody thing!'

In 1963, Les was further promoted to the 'Perth link' which was overnight work on the heavy sleeping car trains right through to Perth, lodging there for the day before returning the following night. Hard work, but lucrative as it was nearly 300 miles each way and the crews were paid an extra hour for each 10 miles over 140 in the shift – later changed to 190. He says that they would fill the box up before leaving shed, then take on an extra couple of tons of coal to ensure enough good hard coal for the return as the softer coal they would receive at Perth was inferior. That way by the time they got to Carlisle on the return journey they would be down to the hard stuff in time for the climb to Shap. Perth would pinch their engine while they were resting and run it to Dundee or Aberdeen – on one occasion they failed their Duchess and provided them with a 'Clan' for the return sleeper which was not appreciated!

Les admitted that the Duchesses were prone to slip, especially as mileage since Works overhaul grew and the engines became out of balance. A slip on starting, especially when the firebox was full, could liven the fire up, but it was more serious on the climbs to Grayrigg, Shap and Beattock in misty or wet weather. He remembered being checked at crucial locations like Harthope halfway up Beattock Bank and the variation between the Duchesses, some getting back into their stride without a slip, others needing nursing. Les admits to talking to his engines, especially in these tricky situations, giving the engine some sotto-voice encouragement.

I'll now use Les Jackson's own words describing a typical Perth run. He called his story 'A Duchess Experience'.

It's late winter 1963 and we are standing at platform 2 at Crewe station, ready to work *The Royal Highlander* (Euston – Inverness) as far as Perth, some 300 miles non-stop. A fresh loco was changed at Crewe and will be changed again at Perth as the train has still 81 miles to go worked by Perth footplate men.

My driver is Len Basford, a good mate with over 48 years' service and with nerves of steel. He was a speed merchant and had an uncanny way of knowing the engine's mood. Our engine tonight is one of Crewe North's best, Duchess 46248 *City of Leeds*. The tender is stacked with ten tons of coal and a fireman's friend, the coal pusher, saves a lot of hard work if it works ok. If not, it means going into the tender to pull coal forward manually, so one must be aware not to climb above cab height or you might hit a bridge and if it's raining, it's not a very nice way to spend a few hours. The cleaners have filled the firebox with about two tons of coal (worth a bribe to do it) and our train tonight is over 610 tons with seventeen coaches including twelve-wheeled sleeping coaches.

We are now ready to depart at 10.25pm, so I open the damper, steam pressure is 240psi, boiler water is just below the top of the glass. If any higher the engine could prime with this load. The station staff give us the green light, as the train is that long we cannot see the guard. I close the firebox door to about two inches to save the glare and put the exhaust injector on and set it on number 3. If it works okay you can leave it on all night and just alter the setting when the engine is working hard, like climbing Shap, etc. Or put on 'max' when the driver closes the regulator to try to stop the engine blowing off 250psi, wasting steam and water and your effort. When four safety valves are blowing, this soon gets the water dropping down the glass, so I try to keep around 235psi all night – it can be done with a good engine.

Len has now opened the regulator and after a short pause, as if to get the bit between his teeth, we are on the move, 'next stop Perth with a bit of luck' says Len. We are now crossing the North Junction where she slipped, but Len was already checking the little dance…the beat of the four cylinders are now getting stronger, we are doing 25mph. Cut-off set at 45 per cent and Len now puts the regulator into second valve up into the roof and puts the cut-off at 35 per cent. It's time for work! I open the fire hole door and look with half closed eyes to save getting blinded by the white hot glow, and the heat is terrific but not warm for the driver as he is hanging out all the way to Perth in the freezing cold. I start a steady firing rate to keep the box full, glance at the water gauge every few minutes, all is well with a full glass. Steam is 240psi and firing is mostly non-stop. If you sit down fifteen minutes in the six hour run you will be lucky! Drink and food is taken between shovels of coal. Even the shovel handle is now hot and the blade hisses when you put it in the wet coal – that is why I wear gloves. We are now well on our way, just past Lancaster and picking up water on Hest Bank troughs. We are on the level, speeding in the high 80s towards Carnforth. This is where the real work begins, and to make matters worse, we are heading into the teeth of a snow storm and gale force winds. Not to worry, we have seen it all before and we have a masterpiece in the Duchess and an expert driver so what more confidence does one need!

The firing rate has now increased, such is the demand for steam. I alter the exhaust injector to 5 to try to keep the water at the top of the glass. We are now passing Oxenholme into the bank proper so now Len drops the cut-off to 30 per cent and still in second valve. It is then that you seem to have feelings for the engine - you have to have steam in the blood, and like a steam fanatic you start talking to her, 'come on, old girl'. I know it's only metal but over the years I have found if you treat them ok, and that includes Electrics, it pays dividends.

We are now speeding towards Tebay and Dillicar water troughs and I hope they are not frozen! Up through the rock cutting we drop the scoop and as we pass over the river bridge, lift the scoop. One had to learn little landmarks which were helpful in bad weather, like now in a snow storm. The rails are now covered. Len asked, 'are you ok, do we need a banker?' 'No, everything ok,' I replied. Any driver worth his salt thinks it against his skill to have one.

We are now into Shap Bank hoping we do not get stopped at Scout Green. But things do not always go to plan! 46248 is now digging into the bank at Scout Green, the exhaust is deafening, and Len has altered the cut-off to 40%. Anyone standing at the lineside could not fail to be filled with emotion, to see such a machine pounding away, the smoke from the exhaust 50ft into the night sky, the glare from the firebox stabbing the sky like some giant searchlight. The fireman is now shovelling coal into the hungry box like a conveyor belt, such is the demand for steam. Water in the glass is now half, so I have increased the exhaust injector setting to 7, the steam gauge is 230psi. 'Come on, old girl, two miles to go and then you can have a short breather.' We are now into the rock cutting 500 yards short of Shap Summit – hope it's not blocked with snow. Len puts the steam sanders on and places his hand on the regulator and within 30 seconds 46248 slipped, but Len was ready (he told me later when I asked 'how did you know?' he said 'I had a premonition' of which I have found out later in life). The cut-off was now 55 per cent as we laboured past Shap Summit signal box at 27mph, but despite our gallant effort from engine and train crew, the summit and raging storm had beat us…we were three minutes late at the top. We had to get that back, we do not like running late. We stormed down the bank towards Penrith and Carlisle at 86mph in places (no speed restriction on sleeper coaches in them days).

We are now past Carlisle and just picked up more water on Floriston trough which is on top of a river bridge. On approaching Kirtlebridge box, Len asked, 'are you ok for Beattock, it's a killer.' If not, we have to crow whistle on passing the box to indicate we need a banker at Beattock. We said we will risk it, hoping the snow plough has been out. We are now through Beattock into the 1 in 75 climb for approx ten miles. Our cut-off is 35 per cent and Len is increasing it very slowly. If too sudden it might make 6248 lose her feet and that would be a test of skill from a standing start. Some engines with the same load would not do it. That's knowing the ability of the engine from the start.

We are past Stirling and Bridge of Allan and on the last lap and bank, getting tired now and shovelling in a trance, every joint aching, legs like jelly, black as panda and longing for a warm bed. It's been a rough night and the fire is now getting dirty and clinkered up. I had to use the dart a time or two but managed to keep the water well up and steam at 225psi on the last few miles past Hilton Junction box into the tunnel and past Perth MPD on the left. Into the station and get relieved for the depot. It's a funny feeling when you step down onto the platform after a non-stop run…

anyone who has not felt the power of the wheels under your feet and rolling at speed has missed the thrill of a lifetime! When we walked away from the engine after being relieved I always turn and look back with a lump in the throat and take another look at the best thing ever invented by man! How much longer will we have them? Little did I know that in 1996 I would be driving 46229 on her last main line run on the northbound *Royal Scot* on my last day before retirement.

Les was the driver, with Graham Massey as fireman, on the epic Shap trials in October 1995, but on the A4 pacific 60007 *Sir Nigel Gresley*, not on Duchess 46229. The A4 may have been the speediest but the Duchess had the power advantage, although on that occasion, as 46229 had some intermittent injector problems, the rejuvenated 71000 *Duke of Gloucester* took the honours. The restoration team of that engine have clearly performed wonders as the comments of my three Crewe drivers on their experiences of firing 71000 in the late 1950s and early 1960s are hardly fit for

Both Neil Cadman and Les Jackson spoke particularly highly of 6248 – 46248 *City of Leeds*, a Crewe North engine which they said was a particularly strong and reliable one. Here it is inside Crewe North shed, c1960. (B. Dobbs/MLS Collection)

Below left: 46248 *City of Leeds* again, at Crewe North depot, c1962. (MLS Collection)

Below right: **On shed** at Crewe North, two of the depot's Duchesses slumbering on shed during the day ready for the night runs to Glasgow and Perth, c1962. (MLS Collection)

Crewe North's 46254 *City of Stoke-on-Trent* about to go off shed passing Camden's 46245 *City of London* which has arrived overnight from Euston on a sleeper train, 1962. (MLS Collection)

printing! It was certainly never allocated to the hard Perth engine diagram turns.

A year later Les Jackson was driver with Firemen Bob Hart and Frank Santrian on 46229 on its last run before withdrawal as its boiler certificate was ending. The train was 11 vehicles 393/427 tons plus class 47 diesel cut inside, 47772 plus support coach, giving a total gross tonnage of 547 tons behind the drawbar. I'll let Les tell his story, which he simply calls 'The final run'.

It's a cold frosty day on 30 November 1996. We are standing in Crewe platform 12 waiting to depart with 46229 *Duchess of Hamilton* on the northbound *Royal Scot*. We have a load of eleven coaches plus a dead class 47 next to the engine to provide train heat. The health and safety powers won't allow us to put steam through, in case a pipe burst in the train. I ask you!

It's my final day at work. I started on steam and I'm going to finish my career on steam! The crowds are gathered round the locomotive as it is also going into retirement because the boiler certificate expires the next day when it gets to York. But first we have Shap, Carlisle, Beattock bank and Glasgow to overcome. I will drive her as far as Carlisle. The train was run by 'Days Out Limited' owned by Mel Chamberlain. The signal has now cleared to green, 46229 has a full head of steam, a green flag from the guard and I put the reverser into full head gear, sound the whistle and open the regulator. A short wheel spin, as if to say let's get at the task ahead, no use being nostalgic as it all has to end sometime. So with a heavy heart we are on the move, no more will I leave Crewe. I don't want it to end.

Then I thought, let's enjoy it and go out in style.

We are now passing Crewe Coal Yard Signal Box. I have pulled the reversing lever to 25 per cent and put the regulator into second valve. We are going like a rocket, such a good engine, she is making light work of it. We speed past Warrington in the 80s and soon have arrived at Preston on time. There is a booked stop for two minutes, then the next stop was Barton loop for water. We left Barton some 22 minutes late. I thought this won't do! On my last day she is going to go like the clappers from here. I will be on time at Carlisle. Luckily I have a friend on the train called Mike Notley who was timing the train and gave me a good log of the run.

We are running alongside the M6 motorway and there are not many cars passing us! The noise from the front end is deafening, the cut-off at 30 per cent and the regulator up in the roof! We speed past Lancaster in a blur and on to Carnforth at over 80. We are now passing milepost 13 near Milnthorpe station. This is where the real work begins, fifteen miles or so of hard climbing to Grayrigg loop. Near the M6 motorway bridge I have two firemen on, one volunteered to stay on from Barton loop.... both shovelling like a conveyor belt. Oxenholme station was like a blur around the 70 mark and the cut-off at 35 per cent, black smoke approx 50ft into the cold sky, spectators by the score on the platform, in the fields, lineside, all the way to Shap Summit. 46229 must have made a lovely sight.

Cut-off now increased to 40 per cent near Lambrigg Crossing, but even with two firemen steam was down to 190psi and we had both injectors on. The water was half a glass, one injector could not keep the boiler topped up as we reached Grayrigg at just over the 50 mark. I was forced to close the regulator and coast down towards Tebay, otherwise we would have had no steam or water for Shap. At Tebay near the old MPD I put the regulator into second valve, cut-off at 25 per cent. My two firemen had worked wonders…. They had got 46229's steam pressure up to 240psi and nearly a full glass of water and with black smoke filling the cold, snowy mountain tops, we hit the bank at 37mph increasing to about 50mph. At the white house, looking back along the train, the exhaust was still hanging half a mile behind the train, the air being that cold. There were spectators by the hundreds each side of the line from Scout Green, cheering us on. I felt quite proud and thought it's not too bad after all. At Scout Green I altered the cut-off to 45 per cent, dropping the wheel down slowly from Tebay North IB otherwise she might slip at Shap Wells. I dropped the cut-off to 55 per cent. Speed was about 42mph and the noise was deafening. Steam was at 220psi but the water was the trouble. I had to put the live steam injector on as we were down to half a glass, not far from the summit now, and just like my old driver Len Basford from years ago on the *Royal Highlander,* I had a premonition she would slip. I put the steam sanders on and placed my hand on the regulator and as we went into the rock cutting some five hundred yards from the summit full of snow and ice, I thought it's now or never and at the white house on the left she gave a good slip, so I shut off and opened up right away again. She held her feet and went over the top at 34mph. On looking at my watch I had twenty minutes to cover the thirty miles to Carlisle to be on time. I said to my firemen, 'hang on, we are going from here!'

Cut-off now back to 25 per cent as we speed around the tight curves at 85 near Penrith. Once past Penrith cut-off was increased to 35 per cent and the speed rose quickly. According to the speedometer she touched 100mph twice!! The last thrill of a lifetime ends too soon as we are now running into Carlisle, according to the time log 4 seconds early and regained 22 minutes late start from Barton loop! Mike also did say the fastest train of the day in BR days was the northbound *Caledonian* booked 69 minutes from passing Lancaster with 245 tons. *We* did it in 64 minutes with a combined weight of over 600 tons ! If the engine had not been eased at Grayrigg to recover steam and water it would have been under the hour.

I got relieved at Carlisle and when I stepped down onto the platform I got a good reception and also met Jill, the real 'Duchess of Hamilton'. I was full with emotion to think that I will never drive a steam locomotive on the main line again. As I walked away and looked back at such a lovely machine I said, 'thanks for a good trip.' It did ease the pain a little and reminded me of many a happy time, both good and the not so good. The next time I hope to see 46229 will be at York with the streamline casing on in the museum.

I understand from my conversation with Les that the Duchess presented him with a memorial plaque to commemorate the run and his retirement and, as he retired once he stepped off the engine, there was nothing the authorities could do about his excess over the locomotive's speed limit. Mike Notley confirmed speed around the 96-97 mark rather than the 100 on 46229's speedometer. I show an outline of Mike Notley's detailed log of Les Jackson's run below:

Crewe-Carlisle, 30 November 1996

46229 *Duchess of Hamilton*

11chs + 47772 (unpowered) 513/547 tons

The Royal Scot **(Days Out Ltd)**

Miles	Location	Times	Speeds		Gradients
0	Crewe	00.00		4¼ L	
7.5	Winsford	11.00	55	3¼ L	Slow Line
11.8	Hartford	14.55	75		
16.5	Weaver Junction	18.36	78½ /75	1¾ L	
21.2	Moore	22.16	81		
24.1	Warrington	24.31	82/74	¾ L	
27.5	Winwick Junction	27.19	69/72		1/132 R
35.9	Wigan	37.58	sigs17*	¾ E	
38.1	Boars Head	42.29	36½		1/104 R
	Coppull Hall Sdg	-	47		1/119 R
44.2	Balshaw Lane	49.10	70	¼ L	1/114 F
51	Preston	58.12	sigs 14*	1½ E	
0		00.00		2 E	
4.65	Barton Loop	12.23		½ L	
0		00.00		20¾ L	
4.1	Garstang	06.59	68½		L
	Bay Horse	-	78		
16.4	Lancaster	16.42	70/80	17½ L	
	Hest Bank	-	84		L
21.5	Carnforth	21.11	82	17 L	
25.7	MP 9 ½	23.44	73½		1/134 R
	Milnthorpe	-	80/75		L, 1/173 R

Crewe-Carlisle, 30 November 1996

46229 *Duchess of Hamilton*

11chs + 47772 (unpowered) 513/547 tons

The Royal Scot **(Days Out Ltd)**

Miles	Location	Times	Speeds		Gradients
35.2	Oxenholme	31.34	65	12½ L	1/111 R
	Hay Fell	-	59		1/131 R
	Lambrigg Crossing	-	58/56		1/106 R
42.2	Grayrigg	39.02	48		1/106 R
48.4	Tebay	47.50	35	13½ L	L, 1/146 R
	Scout Green	-	48/37		1/75 R
53.7	Shap Summit	56.07	35/32		1/75 R
	Thrimby Grange	-	80		1/125 F
	Eden Valley Jn	-	76/85		1/125 F
67.6	Penrith	68.19	73*	12¼ L	
72.4	Plumpton	71.38	91		1/186 F
	Calthwaite	-	96		1/164 F
78.1	Southwaite	75.31	92		1/228 F
	Wreay	-	85/88		1/131 F
<u>85.4</u>	<u>Carlisle</u>	<u>83.09</u>		<u>T</u>	

Above left: **46229** *Duchess of Hamilton*, the class 47 inside and not working, on Les Jackson's last run, passing Oubeck as the light begins to fade, 30 November 1996. (Kevin Truby)

Above right: **Fireman Frank** Santrian, Driver Les Jackson on arrival of the charter *Royal Scot* at Carlisle, 30 November 1996. The lady holding the brochure is the 'real' Duchess of Hamilton who had presented Les with a commemorative plaque when he retired. (Gordon Heddon's Collection)

Neil Cadman

Neil Cadman joined the railway at Macclesfield depot in 1952 and transferred to Crewe North in 1954, allocated as was normal initially to the link known as the 'Block' covering a miscellaneous number of duties. By 1959 he was in the Glasgow link and six months later on the Perth night sleeper trains – this would be during the summer months at first, as with a reduced number of services in the winter timetable the junior crews in the link would step back to the Glasgow and London day turns and trains like the night Postal. Neil's first turn firing a pacific was to Glasgow on the night Postal, although it was on a 'Princess Royal', 46206 *Princess Marie Louise*. He was fortunate it was that one, as it was the only one of the class fitted with a tender coal-pusher, 'the fireman's friend'. His driver, having established he'd not fired a wide firebox pacific before, just said, 'Can you do what you're told? Just keep the back corners full,' advice that was essential for the Duchesses too. Neil recounted a number of his more memorable trips with Duchesses. In the summer of 1959, he was firing the second of the two Ivatt Duchesses built in 1948 – 46257 *City of Salford*. They were on the day Perth-Euston, running up from Crewe, booked just under three hours for the 158 miles, but including copious recovery time. His driver was Eric Hardman, and he remembered passing Harrow & Wealdstone with the speed recorder fluctuating around 102mph. 'A lovely engine,' he said, 'very free-running with its roller bearings and riding very smoothly.'

Then in the summer of 1960 he remembered being fireman to Albert Shaw who was himself the fireman on the *Coronation* in July 1937 when it touched 113 or 114mph approaching Crewe. This time, however, it was on the Up *Midday Scot*, changing engines at Crewe. He had 46225 *Duchess of Gloucester* and despite the electrification checks, arrived early in Euston in 171 minutes from Crewe. In the bleak winter of 1962, he had a very memorable experience. He and Driver Len Basford, mentioned also by Les Jackson, were on the 5.40pm departure from Glasgow, due at Crewe at 50 minutes past midnight. The weather was atrocious with heavy snow and visibility in the darkness and driving snow was poor. They had 46244 *King George VI* and running at about 70mph on the approach to Beattock summit, somewhere around Lamington, they suddenly slammed into something on the line, both being flung across the cab, suffering severe bruising. Their shriek of alarm was because they feared they had hit a preceding train. For a few moments as the train decelerated severely to less than 30mph they were totally disorientated and bewildered until they realised they had ploughed into a giant snowdrift – amazing that it could cause a 600-700 ton projectile to lose 40mph in a hundred yards. The weight and stability of the Duchess paid off and they were miraculously not derailed. They were the last train through. The line was subsequently closed for a week until the snow had been cleared. Later that summer, Neil was back in the Perth link and one night his turn took him through to Euston leaving Crewe at 4.10am. By this time many of the night services were hauled by the Type 40 English Electric 2,000hp diesels, but they had Upperby's 46250 *City of Lichfield*. The arrival of Duchesses on the heavy overnight services in London was rare by the late summer of 1963, and on arrival at Euston around 7.45am, it was surrounded by admiring contract workers involved in the demolition and rebuilding of the old station. Euston station by then resembled a bomb site and looking at the size and brooding power of the pacific, one of the contractors remarked that it could probably save them a lot of trouble by attaching a steel chain and dragging the rest of the old edifice down. Camden shed had been closed by this time, so they had to take 46250 out to Willesden for servicing before returning to Crewe.

Neil mentioned that he, like Les Jackson and a number of Crewe firemen, would fill the box up with coal before leaving shed, and then take on another couple of tons of coal to maximise the usage of the good hard coal used by Crewe North and act as insurance if they had a hard trip or were badly delayed – it was not unknown for a Duchess on a heavy sleeper from Perth to run out of coal on the return and have to hook off at Carlisle or Preston to top up to complete the turn. Bill Andrew challenged this, saying he kept the fire thin, although ensuring the back corners of the firebox were properly covered. He liked to start from Crewe with a good bright hot fire, he considered it more efficient. It would take a Duchess with a full box some time to burn through which could lead to slower starts from Crewe. What seems remarkable was that the Duchesses thrived from various methods of both firing and driving. They were tolerant engines and always seemed to have much in reserve.

Bill Andrew

Bill Andrew started his footplate career at Rose Grove and moved to Crewe North in 1956. He remembers his first firing turn on a Duchess was on Christmas Eve 1957 when the booked fireman failed to turn up. It was the first of the night sleepers to Perth, with sixteen on. He remembers being at Stirling at 4 o' clock in the morning and being amazed to see the Northern Lights in the sky. He was so exhausted he slept for ten hours while his engine was used by Perth shed for a run to Dundee or Aberdeen and back, before he and his mate booked on for a return sleeper the next night. He got the Perth men who prepared the engine to shovel the Perth 'cobbles' forward so that the best Yorkshire hard coal would surface later and fired steadily without respite until the heavy sleeper had surmounted the 1 in 100 to Gleneagles. Like Neil, he progressed from the 'Block' to the Glasgow link, actually a year earlier in 1958, which meant runs to London also. London men had the 8-coach flyers, Carlisle Upperby men had the day Perth turns, but Crewe had the Postal, some of the night sleepers and the heavy *Midday Scot*. When he joined Neil and Les in the Perth link, they would have a couple of lodging turns to Perth

Bill Andrew and Neil Cadman at Crewe Heritage Centre in front of the preserved record-breaking APT, 21 July 2021. (David Maidment)

During the day long layover at Perth after hauling the overnight sleeper from Crewe, 46234 *Duchess of Abercorn* gets some unconventional topping up with coal during problems at the coaling stage, 27 May 1958. (J.A. Peden/MLS Collection)

in the week, filling in with lighter turns in between – London and back, or the North Wales Coast or a running in turn to Shrewsbury or Manchester and back. One of the Crewe turns that was particularly demanding was the *Royal Highlander* sleeper, not only because it regularly loaded sixteen or seventeen heavy sleeper cars but also because it was non-stop between Crewe and Motherwell, with no respite or short rest to pull things round.

Both Neil and Les had a favourite Duchess – 46248 *City of Leeds*. On the other hand, Bill Andrew said they were all good, though like all engines they were best after Works overhauls until their mileage ran up – because of their work the Crewe and Camden engines accumulated mileage quickly and would amass 75,000 miles in the year necessitating an annual Works visit. Bill remembered 46235 *City of Birmingham* in particular which was a Crewe North engine for its entire career, but reiterated that they were all good. The coal-pusher was particularly valued by the firemen on these long runs, though Bill said that you had to resist the pressure to operate it too early in the run, as the weight of coal in a near full tender could stress the machine and cause it to fail. On the London runs, especially the *Midday Scot* diagram, they often got 71000 and both Les and Neil expressed their frustration with the engine and its poor steaming reputation compared with the Stanier pacifics. It was not by chance that it was never allocated to Crewe's Perth turns. On one occasion Bill said he did have it unusually on a Glasgow run and he fired it as he would on a Duchess, firing steadily but trying to keep a thin fire. The engine performed well and they had a good trip but there was no coal left in the tender when they got back to Crewe!

By the winter of 1962 the class 40 diesels were in charge of the majority of the heavy turns, though they were not as powerful as the Duchesses on Shap or Beattock. However, the prolonged freeze that winter caused many diesel failures and the Duchesses were out in force for a few weeks. In discussion between the drivers, the reserve of power that the Duchesses possessed was a major factor, power that was rarely fully utilised. Much work could be performed on the first valve of the regulator and cut-off at 15 or 20 per cent. Bill said that he rarely used more than 35 per cent even on the steepest banks. He reckoned that the Duchesses used about 50 gallons of water to the mile and in his view the tenders provided with only 4,000 gallon capacity was not enough. He would try to avoid letting the engine blow off steam for every time the safety valves lifted, he estimated that he was wasting ten gallons of water a minute. The problem was that a larger tender would push the length of the Duchess beyond the capacity of most of the LMS turntables. When the Manchester London Road turntable was removed in the electrification work in 1959, any Duchess visiting Manchester had to turn on the Buxton/Daventry Junction 'Khyber' triangle as the Longsight turntable could only take a 4-6-0.

Like Les Jackson, Bill Andrew elected to work steam specials as a driver, and finished his career employed by the West Coast company at Carnforth where in the first decade of the twenty-first century he teamed up frequently with 6233 *Duchess of Sutherland*, which for many years had been a Crewe North engine, though it finished at Edge Hill. He remembered one 'scary' moment with 6233 when on a charter train, they lost the use of the exhaust injector in the Lune Gorge and then the live steam injector packed up at Tebay. There was now a real danger of 'dropping a plug' on Shap, so they stopped at Scout Green halfway up the 1 in 75, and eventually got the water flow going, avoiding having to drop the fire. After a twenty minute stand, Bill managed to restart the train (13 coach load) and cleared the summit at 25mph.

Bill sent me a couple of pages from *Steam Railway* magazine where Mike Notley described a record run he had timed on 4 September 2004 over Grayrigg and Shap with a 12-coach 455 ton gross load. 6233 had averaged 74.8mph between Winsford and Moore but the run from Warrington to Preston was beset by signal checks and despite 77mph at Hest Bank, the train was six minutes late at Carnforth. It was drizzling when they set out after the water stop and would prove a test of the Duchess's reputation of slipping. Bill took things gently up the 1 in 134 to MP 9½, passed at 36mph, accelerated to 69 at Hincaster Junction and passed Oxenholme at 58½mph having already cut nearly five minutes off an absurdly easy schedule. A summary of Mike Notley's log over the fells is shown below:

Miles	Location	Times	Speed		Gradient
0	Carnforth	00.00		T	
13.1	Oxenholme	17.23	58	4¾ E	1/111 R
14	MP 20	18.18	54		1/104 R
16	Hay Fell	20.32	52		1/131 R
18	Lambrigg Crossing	23.16	47½		1/106 R
20	Grayrigg	25.38	42		1/106 R
26.2	Tebay	31.22	77	8¾ E	L, 1/146 R
28	MP 34	32.53	63		1/75 R
29	Scout Green	33.53	55		1/75 R
31.2	Shap Summit	36.40	42		1/75 R

With a maximum of 78mph through Eden Valley Junction, Penrith was passed a full fourteen minutes early and with nothing over 70mph afterwards, arrival at Carlisle was 21¾ minutes early (68 minutes 20 seconds for the 63.1 miles from Carnforth). The time for the Shap climb – 5¾ miles from MP 31¼ (just before Tebay) to the summit – was 5 minutes 52 seconds, a new record for a twelve coach train. The fireman was Graeme Bunker and Mike Notley reported that 6233 was observed to be blowing off steam as it topped Grayrigg. Despite the weather, there was not a trace of a slip noticeable from the train.

I find I had a run behind 6233 with Bill Andrew at the regulator back in 2002 which I recounted among my own reminiscences in the previous chapter. Bill did well again on a special charter, the Royal Touring Company's *Royal Scot*, on 10 October 2009. 6233 worked the special both ways between Crewe and Carlisle. The load was a much heavier thirteen coaches plus diesel 57601 attached to the rear of the train. The tare weight including that of the 'dead' diesel was 585 tons, 625 gross. The diesel-hauled train arrived ten minutes late at Crewe and the train was routed on the slow line as far as Hartford losing a further four minutes. Bill Andrew, supported by his regular (and equally-aged) fireman, Frank Santrian, and assisted by Simon Scot from the Princess Royal Class Locomotive Trust, gradually trimmed the lateness back and arrived at the water stop, Carnforth, only six minutes late. Further time was recovered there and the *Royal Scot* left just 1½ minutes late. Initially 6233 primed and the Duchess fell from 39 to 30½mph on the 1 in 134 to MP 9½ and this low speed had an impact at the start of the 13 mile climb to Grayrigg. The climb in earnest was begun at 65mph and by Oxenholme on the 1 in 111 speed was down to 53mph. The climb outline was:

Miles	Location	Times	Speed		Gradient
0	Carnforth	00.00		1½ L	
13.1	Oxenholme	18.10	53	2¾ L	1/111 R
14	MP 20	19.10	51		1/104 R
16	Hay Fell	-	40		1/131 R
18	Lambrigg Crossing	-	38/39		1/106 R
20	Grayrigg	28.08	37½		1/106 R

The two fireman were working continuously to supply the required steam and Bill was able to take advantage of the level section through the Lune Valley, reaching 70mph before Dillicar troughs and a maximum of 74½ just before Tebay. The run continued:

Miles	Location	Times	Speed		Gradient
26.2	Tebay	34.13	73	2¾ L	L, 1/146 R
28	MP 34	35.47	61½		1/75 R
29.1	Scout Green	37.01	51½		1/75 R
31.2	Shap Summit	40.00	35½		1/75 R

Doug Landau, another of my colleagues from the Bevils Club mentioned earlier, calculated an indicated horsepower of over 2,700 on the lower part of the climb to Shap and it actually beat the 1939 test with 6234 *Duchess of Abercorn* by over half a minute between Tebay and Shap Summit with fifteen tons greater load. After that it was plain sailing and an easy run down to Carlisle achieved a 1½ minute early arrival with a time of 71 minutes for the 63.1 miles from Carnforth. Bill Andrew, like other drivers of these charter trains, received many photographs of them in action and he has given me a number from which to make a selection to illustrate this part of the book, which should be read in conjunction with the next chapter which describes the preservation, restoration and operation of the three remaining Duchesses – 6229, 6233 and 6235.

6233 *Duchess of Sutherland* on the *Royal Scot* charter train at Shap Summit, Bill Andrew at the cab window, 9 October 2008. (Howard Routledge/Bill Andrew Collection)

6233 passing Lancaster with *The Shap Duchess* on 4 September 2004. It bore the *Caledonian* headboard to mark the 40th anniversary of the last run of the *Caledonian* London – Glasgow Express of 4 September 1964. (Bill Andrew Collection)

6233 *Duchess of Sutherland* at Preston with a charter train for Blackpool North, 10 May 2008. (Bill Andrew Collection)

106 • THE LMS PRINCESS CORONATION PACIFICS, THE FINAL YEARS & PRESERVATION

6233 *Duchess of Sutherland* on the charter *Citadel Express* to Carlisle climbing Shap near Scout Green, 18 April 2009.
(Eddie Bobrowski/Bill Andrew Collection)

6233 passing the photographer on the *Citadel Express* at Scout Green, 18 April 2009.
(Eddie Bobrowski/Bill Andrew Collection)

Railwaymen remember • 107

Above left: **6233 breasting** Shap Summit with the *Royal Scot* charter train, 10 October 2009. (Bill Andrew Collection)

Above right: **Bill Andrew** peering from the cab of 6233 on the *Royal Scot* charter during its northbound run to Carlisle, 10 October 2009. (Bill Andrew Collection)

6233 leaning to the curve through Penrith station, returning to Crewe with the *Royal Scot* charter train, 10 October 2009. (Roger Bastin/Bill Andrew Collection)

108 • THE LMS PRINCESS CORONATION PACIFICS, THE FINAL YEARS & PRESERVATION

A portrait of Driver Bill Andrew on the footplate of 6233 after its repaint in LMS lined black livery, 2010. (Dave Hurd/Bill Andrew Collection)

6233 on the climb to Shap Summit with a charter train in 2010 with the *Citadel Express* headboard.
(Bill Andrew Collection)

6233 climbing to Ais Gill at Kirkby Stephen on the *Cumbrian Mountain Express*, 28 August 2010. (Howard Routledge/Bill Andrew Collection)

Keith J. Collier

Keith joined the railway at Crewe Works in 1955 and was an apprentice there spending much time in No.10 (the Erecting Shop) and was a fitter in the last three or so years of the major overhauls of the Duchess pacifics which ceased at Crewe in 1962. By the time of the diesel electric Type 4s (class 40) he was a Chargeman Fitter with fifty-one men under his command. His work on the Duchesses included the critical job of fitting the motion after repair. He would be fitting the left hand motion simultaneously with another fitter working on the right hand side. By and large the Duchesses would be in relatively sound condition when they came in for their heavy overhauls. Most of their duties did not unduly stretch them and they were strong robust machines. All seemed good machines although when pushed Keith admitted that 46255 *City of Hereford* did have a slightly poorer reputation. It spent most of its life at Carlisle and seemed rarely to be seen on the most prestigious trains. Working on them was fairly straightforward apart from adjusting the inside motion which was in restricted space and difficult to reach. Lining up the slidebars was a 'cheesewire' job.

If a Duchess did not need a repair requiring lifting the boiler, or a repaired spare boiler was available, a full overhaul could be done in a three-week period. Otherwise, it could take many more weeks – a problem that afflicted 71000 as its boiler was unique.

I asked Keith about some of the more irksome jobs on the Duchesses. At a heavy general repair, the refurbished pistons would be fitted together and both front and rear cylinder covers. In those days, no joints or gaskets were allowed anywhere on a steam engine with all steam tight joints being face to face. If a joint blew out especially on a footplate valve for example, it could be catastrophic for the footplate crew. So the cylinder covers were fitted face to face with a coating on the faces of 'boiled oil'.

The crosshead was fitted and it was here that a very important first measurement was taken. At this time there was no con rod fitted so the piston was bump stopped by hand to first the front cylinder cover and then the rear cylinder cover. When the piston was bumped up to the front cover for example a standard 4 inch trammel was used to scribe a point on the top slide bar from a centre pop on the cross head and the same when the piston was bumped up to the rear cylinder cover. Both scribed marks on the slide bar would then be 'centre popped'. These centre pop marks would be used later when the valve gear, etc. was being fitted.

The Duchess was then lifted with the overhead cranes and dropped onto the driving wheels only with the front bogie and bissel truck fitted later. Once placed on the driving wheels, only the trailing set would be coupled up to the springs, etc., with the rest of the engine supported on screw jacks. This left the leading and intermediate driver completely free in the axle box horns. Roller tackle was now fitted to the two free driving wheels and were lifted just clear of the track by this tackle so the wheels could be revolved on these rollers by a compressed air driven motor. On the Duchess the outside con rods would be fitted together with all the valve gear coupled up so that when the wheels were rotated the valve events could be accurately set with its associated tackle for the job.

It was then that during the valve setting the previously centre popped crossheads and slide bars were used for critical piston to cylinder cover clearances. Each piston was stopped at both front and rear dead centres and the same standard four inch trammel was used to check the now different scribed position on the slide bars which should be 5/16 of an inch. This was a critical measurement as it was part of the designed total clearance volume and also to make sure the covers were not hit by the pistons especially if a big end went allowing the con rod to travel a little further.

It was here that a most disagreeable job could occur on the inside cylinders if for example the trammel measurement showed incorrect clearance between a piston and a rear cylinder cover so the piston would have to come out for skimming or in some cases the back cylinder cover had to come off for machining. This would mean taking down the inside con rod, splitting the crosshead from the piston, taking down the slide bars, removing both front and rear cylinder covers, removing the piston and then mauling the rear cover down with a scaffolding tube through the cover piston gland hole. Within the tight confines inside the frames this was a most disagreeable task. On top of this there was no electric lead lamps in those steam days with illumination provided by candles screwed in a

⅞in Whitworth nut for a candle base. 'Yes, they were the good old days but we got on with it as I'm sure they did at other main works.'

Keith was, however, critical of a number of design aspects of the Duchesses. He felt they were in fact overboiled – the boiler tubes were too long at 19ft 3in for five ⅛in diameter flue tubes which, when filled with the trifurcated superheater elements gave a poor A/S ration of 1/553, the ideal being 1/400. This gave a poor superheat temperature. Indeed, the flue gas cooled so much after traversing the long flue tubes that tests revealed the superheater tubes were actually reheating the flue gas near the smokebox end of the boiler. In Keith's view, the last two Duchesses, 46256 and 46257, were even worse in this respect as their different design of superheater known as FP4s gave an A/S ratio of 1/664. They were later replaced by standard Duchess superheater elements.

The 6ft 9in diameter coupled wheels instead of the 6ft 6in wheels of the 'Princess Royal' was a mistake. Drivers used to say 'take them out in carpet slippers'! In Keith's view, having four cylinders on a big pacific was also a mistake as four cylinder cranks set at 90 degrees gave a very uneven turning moment and can be 24 per cent above the mean value. As a comparison, a three-cylinder engine such as a 'Rebuilt Royal Scot' had a much more even turning movement with only about 8 per cent above the mean value. This poor starting was not helped by the Duchesses having unequal length conrods - the outside at 11ft and inside 8ft 6in. This gave differing angularity between outside and inside engine acceleration, the inside giving greater piston acceleration than the outside engine piston in mid-stroke.

Another less than ideal aspect on these engines was the inside valve driven by the outside valve gear by rocking shafts. The inside radius of the rocking shaft described an arc as it rocked to and fro and could never mirror the inside valve gear with the outside valves. Keith's preference would have been for a three cylinder machine like the rebuilt 'Merchant Navies' - or the Stanier 'Rebuilt Royal Scots' which he felt were better engines than the pacifics, though on the long hauls the larger wide firebox of the pacifics avoided the problem of ash disposal. (J.F. Harrison who came from the Eastern Region after nationalisation had a similar preference for high-powered three cylinder machines.) Ten of the 'Royal Scots' were fitted in 1953/4 with roller bearings on the inside big-ends and Keith was puzzled that no effort was made to equip the Duchesses similarly, especially the last couple built by Ivatt.

He had a fair bit of experience of them on the road as well as on the Works, and stated that they had to be handled very carefully on starting to avoid slipping – open the regulator, then close quickly as it begins to move and then open again slowly. Many drivers felt more confident with a 'Princess Royal' on the banks if the weather was wet, or would be more inclined to request a banker – something my three interviewed drivers would see as an aspersion cast on their skill. The load of the train on the locomotive draw gear tends to pull the cab end of a steam locomotive hard down onto the track, but on a pacific as opposed to a 4-6-0, it is prevented from doing so by the trailing truck. If the design of the trailing truck had long travel coil springs as fitted to 71000 and Bulleid's 'Merchant Navies' it might have alleviated some of this problem. He noticed how many drivers would stack up extra coal. In his view if carefully stacked, he reckoned some drivers managed to stow thirteen tons onto the ten-ton capacity tender! Like the 'Princess Royals', the Duchesses rode well, their bogies easing into the curves. He had experienced 105mph on the footplate of 46251 at the foot of the bank through Beattock station having almost drifted down the bank with little steam provision, but without the usual brake applications to steady the train.

Keith accepts that his critical views of the Duchess design are probably not shared by many others, but being at the sharp end and with his experience of masterminding 71000 back to health he knows that modifications in the design could have improved the Duchesses further. He admitted that when the first Duchess came into Crewe Works to be cut up – he thinks it was probably one of the Camden ones, 46246 *City of Manchester* – he realised that the era of steam was passing and felt quite emotional.

Chapter 6
PRESERVATION

6229 *Duchess of Hamilton*
6229 was built in September 1938 as a maroon streamlined pacific at a cost of £10,136 and was allocated to Crewe North shed. It went to the USA in January 1939 redesignated as 6220 *Coronation*. It returned in March 1942, regained its 6229 identity in 1943 after a Works visit, and averaged around 75,000 miles a year with a peak of 90,994 in 1959, totalling 1,533,846 miles before withdrawal in February 1964. It was then sold to Butlin's for display at their Minehead Holiday Camp and repainted crimson red, with its smoke deflectors removed so it appeared in the form and livery of non-streamlined engines, 6230-6234. It was considered for transfer to the Bressingham Museum in 1970 but 6233 was preferred. The Transport Trust was then requested by Butlin's to seek a home for 6229 as its condition was deteriorating in the sea air. In August 1974, the National Railway Museum expressed interest and negotiated a 20-year loan agreement and arrangements were made with BREL Swindon to carry out restoration to static exhibition standards. It was hauled as far as Taunton by diesel 25 059 on 13 March 1975 after road haulage to the closed Minehead railhead of the branch. It was conducted at slow speed, taking four hours to traverse the closed line which the West Somerset Railway was seeking to acquire at the time.

It was then moved by rail to Swindon Works on 17 March where after consideration of a number of restoration options, a decision was made to restore it as a non-working exhibit in its external condition at the time at a final cost of £17,000. The boiler's blue asbestos lagging was removed and external surfaces treated with anti-corrosive paint. Its smoke deflectors were replaced and it was finished in the late 1950s livery of BR maroon as it had operated during in the final years before its withdrawal. Although restoration at Swindon was mainly cosmetic, there was a lot of descaling and renewal of metalwork and it went on public display in the National Railway Museum at York in 1976. Funds were then raised by the museum to restore it to full working order and the work was supervised by the Museum's Chief Mechanical Engineer, John Bellwood. The boiler tubes and superheater elements were renewed. The main internal copper steam pipe was replaced by one of steel construction welded onto the front tubeplate. The repaired boiler was steam tested at 375lb psi. After several problems were overcome, a hydraulic test on 4 March 1980 was successful and the engine was steamed in April. A lot of hard work had been undertaken by volunteers from York Railway Circle and the North Yorkshire Moors Railway freeing the seized up parts – cylinder draincock, damper, hopper ashpan, rocker grate and injector water feed system. Rust was removed and disintegrated stays replaced. The boiler was relagged by the end of April and in May 1980 a successful test run at 60mph was completed. The first run with passengers was a double run round the York-Leeds-Harrogate-York circuit on 10 May 1980 which revealed that there was still work to be done. The steam leakages became a protracted problem and it was not until the 'Postal Special' in November that 46229's front end was finally steam-tight. It took part in the Rainhill celebrations in May 1980. It then became one of the locomotives in the pool for the Manchester-Liverpool 150th anniversary celebrations, working the official Anniversary Special on 14 September 1980. Its first *Cumbrian Mountain Express* run in November was a disappointment as it stalled on the 'Long Drag', slipping badly in the rain, its steam sanders not coping with the conditions. The following week the southbound run was completed successfully and in the early 1980s 46229 put up a remarkable number of runs on the *Cumbrian Mountain Express* in both directions.

My friend Alastair Wood timed a number of excellent runs with it in the early 1980s. On 23 October 1982 it worked the return *Welsh Marches Pullman*, a 13-coach 494/515 ton train. It stormed the Gresford bank with a minimum of 41mph at the top of the four miles of 1 in 82 and cut four minutes from the Chester-Ruabon timing despite a p-way slack to 15mph at Wrexham. 58½mph on the 1 in 143 through Chirk to Weston Rhyn was followed by steady running at 75-76mph between Gobowen and Shrewsbury. A week later on the 31 November with a similar load it climbed the 1 in 106/95 to Pontypool Road at 41mph and the 1 in 82/95 of Llanvihangel bank at 38/40mph. My own footplate run on 46229 on the Settle & Carlisle route in March 1983 followed as described in chapter 4 and on 29 October 1983 with fourteen coaches, 496/530 tons, it stormed the climb to Blea Moor sustaining 51mph after Horton-in-Ribblesdale, 46 at Ribblehead and 43½ at Blea Moor, arriving at the Garsdale water stop sixteen minutes early. A week later, on the southbound *Cumbrian Mountain Express* with the same load, it held 43mph on the 1 in 100 through Kirkby Stephen until a couple of slips reduced the speed to 38, then it accelerated again to 43mph at Ais Gill. In December 46229 was at it again sustaining 54-52mph on the 1 in 100 to Ribblehead in dank misty conditions before slowing over the viaduct though with a slighter lighter load – thirteen coaches, 452/475 tons. Finally on 7 January 1984 with thirteen coaches, 455/485 tons, it accelerated from 48mph at Griseburn to 55 before Kirkby Stephen, 46 at Birkett Tunnel, 54 at Mallerstang and 53mph minimum at Ais Gill.

In 1985 it moved south to work the BR Sunday lunch *Shakespeare Expresses* from Marylebone. Its boiler certificate expired in October 1985, and it returned to the NRM for overhaul. The cab height was reduced by two inches to allow it to work 'under the wires' and the tank capacity was increased to 5,000 gallons. During the 1990s it ran on a number of heritage railways as well as main line tours, its final main line run before the boiler certificate expired again was on 30 November 1996 when it hauled a *Royal Scot* special over the 401 miles from Euston to Glasgow, returning to York the next day via Edinburgh and the East Coast main line. In 1997 it ran a few photographic charters painted BR green before a final run on the East Lancashire Railway in March 1998, repainted red, and it returned to the NRM by road in September.

It was then the subject of a feasibility study to be rebuilt in the original streamline form and to main line running standards, but the cost was excessive and it returned for static exhibition at the National Railway Museum in 2001, standing next to *Mallard*. In September 2005 the NRM announced that the streamlining would be re-instated, returning the locomotive to its original appearance, although restoration to operational condition was not pursued at this time. This work was to be undertaken at Tyseley Locomotive Works and a committee was set up to raise the cash required and oversee the restoration, with management of the NRM, members of the 229 club (part of Friends of the NRM), Tony Streeter of *Steam Railway* which was sponsoring the work and Bob and Alastair Meanley of Tyseley Works.

46229 was moved from its appearance at the Crewe Works Open Day in September 2005 to Tyseley Works hauled by a class 37 diesel, and the first action there was the fitting of a smokebox upper section and restoring 46229 as a de-streamlined 'semi' painted on one side in LMS 1946 black livery for a brief photographic opportunity. Work was then done to extend streamlining to the rear of the tender which was from 46239 (46229's original had been scrapped with 46239 in 1964). Drawings from the NRM and pre-war photographs from Crewe Works helped the restoration team. The curved front panels were manufactured by Coventry Prototype Panels, a company working in the motor trade, using a wooden mock-up of the front end shaper casing to confirm the shape.

Many problems challenged the team but perhaps the major one was obtaining sheet steel of sufficiently large size for the six feet wide central panels of the casing, and this took months to resolve. Diplomatic assistance finally resulted in an offer of help from Tata Steel and its UK subsidiary Corus of a ton of suitable steel produced at the Llanwern steelworks by the only machine in Europe able to produce sheets in the width required. The re-streamlining was completed under much pressure to meet the NRM launch date of 19 May 2009, being hauled from Tyseley to York the previous day by class 47 No 47773. It then went on display in a new exhibition called 'Duchess of Hamilton Streamlined: Styling An Era'.

114 • THE LMS PRINCESS CORONATION PACIFICS, THE FINAL YEARS & PRESERVATION

Above left: **6229** *Duchess of Hamilton* after returning from the USA in 1942 and seen here at Crewe in 1943 after a Works visit when it regained its correct identity. (Bob Meanley's Collection)

Above right: **46229 seen** at Camden before preservation, June 1963. It was allocated to Edge Hill, Liverpool in its last year, having previously been a Camden engine for many years. (D. Loveday/MLS Collection)

Below: **6229** *Duchess of Hamilton* as restored in LMS maroon livery and without smoke deflectors for Butlin's at Minehead, 12 April 1964. (R.H.G. Simpson/MLS Collection)

Preservation • 115

6229 being hauled away from Minehead by 25059 at Blue Anchor, 13 March 1975. (R.O. Coffin)

6229 under overhaul and restoration for the National Railway Museum, at Swindon Works BREL, 5 November 1975. Note the cab of one of the three Vale of Rheidol narrow gauge tank engines undergoing overhaul alongside. (Brian Morrison)

46229 *Duchess of Hamilton* now restored in BR red livery and seen at the Liverpool-Manchester 150 Anniversary, at Bold Colliery Sidings with other exhibits including 4771 *Green Arrow*, 25 May 1980.
(Peter J.C. Skelton)

46229 *Duchess of Hamilton* on the *Cumbrian Mountain Express* near Dent in the spring of 1983. The author's safety audit run on this train, when he was the LMR Chief Operating Manager, was during this month.
(Author's Collection)

Preservation • 117

Above left: **The NRM's** 46229 *Duchess of Hamilton* near Duffield with the York-Crewe *York Royale* charter train, 8 June 1996. (Trefor Evans)

Above right: **46229** *Duchess of Hamilton* in York National Railway Museum alongside 4468 *Mallard* and part of a Channel Tunnel high speed train cab section, 2001. (Author's Collection)

Below: **The first** steps to 6229's conversion to the streamlined state with the cutting of the smokebox and the fitting of the new 'squashed' smokebox ring at Tyseley Works, April 2006. (Bob Meanley)

Above left: The streamlined extensions to 6229's tender – note the square cut for the 'door' to access the tank for the water column hose. (Bob Meanley)

Above right: The lower half of the streamlining is fitted at Tyseley, May 2008. (Bob Meanley)

Right: Just a month to go before the deadline and 6229's streamlining nears completion as it emerges from Tyseley Works, 12 April 2009. (Bob Meanley)

Preservation • 119

Above left: 6229 on the turntable and about to be shunted into the paint shop at Tyseley Works, 7 May 2009. (Bob Meanley)

Above right: The team that brought about the restreamlining of 6229 posing in front of the displayed locomotive on the first day of its exhibition in this form – from left to right, Don Heath (Friend of the NRM), Jim Rees (NRM), Alastair Meanley (Tyseley Loco Works), Danny Hopkins (editor Steam Railway), Graeme Bunker (Friend of the NRM), Ian Smith (Friend of the NRM), Bob Meanley (Tyseley Loco Works), Helen Ashby (NRM), 19 May 2009.

Below: The completed streamlined 6229 waiting to be taken into the National Railway Museum, May 2009, posing alongside the LNER A4 4489 *Dominion of Canada*, repatriated from the country for the gathering of A4s at the museum later that year. (Bob Meanley Collection)

120 • THE LMS PRINCESS CORONATION PACIFICS, THE FINAL YEARS & PRESERVATION

Above left: **6229** *Duchess of Hamilton* as re-streamlined at Tyseley Works and displayed at the National Rail Museum, 10 December 2021. (David Maidment)

Above right: **The impressive** streamlined front end of 6229 on display at the NRM, 10 December 2021. (David Maidment)

Below left: 6229's tender showing the coal-pusher with a coach from the *Coronation Scot* set at the National Rail Museum, 10 December 2021. (David Maidment)

Below right: 6229's cab controls on display at the NRM, 10 December 2021. (David Maidment)

6233 *Duchess of Sutherland*

6233 was built in July 1938 at a cost of £9,585 plus £1,509 for the tender and the cost was depreciated to nil by 1968 which indicates that a 30-year life was envisaged when authorised. It spent much of its career at Crewe North, finishing at Edge Hill, Liverpool from where it was withdrawn in February 1964, having accumulated 1,657,270 miles. A railway enthusiast, Brian Walker, tried to persuade a number of councils (unsuccessfully) to preserve a Duchess associated with their city and then tried Butlin's, interesting their Assistant Managing Director, G.S. Ogg. Initially the Butlin's Board rejected the idea because of cost, but were subsequently convinced and acquired 46100 for Skegness, 46203 for Pwllheli and after finding the purchase price of GW King 6018 too much, purchased 46229 for Minehead. 46242 *City of Glasgow* was suggested for the Heads of Ayr camp, but in the end 46233 was selected and bought for £2,500 from BR. It was prepared at Crewe Works for the sale and display in June 1964, restoring it to its 1938 condition without smoke deflectors and with single chimney and painted LMS red. It was moved to Ayr in October 1964 and displayed alongside LB&SCR 'Terrier' *Martello* (formerly BR 32662). Its condition deteriorated with corrosion from the sea air and Butlin's decided to release their locomotives in 1970. After initially acquiring 6100 *Royal Scot* for his Bressingham Gardens Museum, Alan Bloom agreed with Butlin's in February 1971 to look after 6233 on a 20-year free loan and it moved there by rail in March. After an initial static display, restoration to running order took place between 1972 and 1974 at a cost of £16,000 and some 19,000 man-hours of work. It was steamed there on a short length of track between 1974 and 1976 and then retired once more as a static exhibit for the following 25 years after firebox defects were discovered requiring expensive repairs.

The Rank company bought Butlin's in 1989 and decided to sell rather than continue the loan of the locomotives and after some difficult negotiations Bressingham bought 6233 for £100,000. It remained at Bressingham until 1993 when it was hired to the East Lancs Railway for a month and the cost of its restoration to running order was estimated at £162,000, too much at that time to undertake. It returned to Bressingham for static display until purchased by the Princess Royal Class Locomotive Trust (PRCLT) headed by Brell Ewart in November 1995 and moved to the Butterley site in January 1996. A heritage lottery grant to cover the restoration to running order for £324,508 was won in 1998 (75% of the estimated cost) and 6233 was restored to operational mode between August 1998 and March 2000. It was equipped with air brakes and the boiler was overhauled at the Severn Valley Workshop at Bridgnorth. The tender had a new top tank increasing the water capacity to 5,000 gallons. A series of tests took place from January 2001 and loaded tests between July and September. To allow it to run on the main line in preservation, 6233 was fitted with Train Protection & Warning System (TPWS) and on-train monitoring recorder (OTMR) equipment, alongside the BR fitted Automatic Warning System (AWS). A final test took place on 10 September 2001 with Railtrack and HMRI present and after obtaining the necessary certification, main line rail tours commenced and the following routes were covered in 2001 and 2002:

Crewe-Holyhead
Bristol-Plymouth
Derby-St Pancras
Euston-Birmingham via GW route
Liverpool-York
Derby-Blackpool
Crewe-Carlisle via Shap
Carlisle-Glasgow
Carlisle-Leeds-Derby via Settle & Carlisle

6233 performed excellently, recording 5½ minutes for the Tebay-Shap Summit section (62.4mph average) in April 2002, and taking an 11 coach train up Beattock at a minimum of 37mph and arriving at Glasgow 42 minutes early in July! It also performed much better over the South Devon banks than its predecessor, 46236, had done in the 1948 locomotive exchanges. In June 2002 it was selected to head the Royal Train, after the Queen's overnight journey from London, between Holyhead and Llanfairpwll (and the rest of the 58 letters) and then in the afternoon from Llandudno Junction to Crewe.

In September 2004 it recorded another 5 ½ minute climb of Shap with 455 tons gross, after a minimum of 42mph at Grayrigg. Tebay was passed at 79mph and the minimum speed at Shap summit was also 42mph. The 63 miles from Carnforth to Carlisle were covered in 68 minutes 20 seconds, a gain of nearly 22 minutes on the schedule. Driver Bill Andrew was assisted by Fireman Alastair Meanley (the oldest and youngest preservation train crews respectively) and Fireman Graeme Bunker. The most astonishing run of all, however, was in 2005 on the East Coast main line, when 6233 was faced with an ambitious schedule for its run to Darlington with a gross load of over 500 tons. The crew was faced with a timing of 70 minutes to Peterborough when the normal schedule in steam days with a lesser load was 80 minutes, and just 38 minutes for the 44 mile racing stretch from York to Darlington, a time for ECML in steam days for trains less than 300 tons, not 500! I table some of the highlights in the table and paragraphs below, a summary from the full logs given to me by Bob Meanley.

King's Cross – Darlington, 23 July 2005

The Talisman Railtour

6233 *Duchess of Sutherland*

13 chs, 472/505 tons

Miles	Location	Times	Speeds		Gradients
0	King's Cross	00.00			
2.4	Finsbury Park	06.37	41	1½ L	1/107 R
12.6	Potters Bar	17.38	54/61½	3½ L	1/200 R
17.5	Hatfield	21.40	80		1/200 F
20.25	Welwyn-Garden-City	23.44	72	2¾ L	1/200 R
25	Knebworth	27.35	74		1/200 R
27.45	Stevenage	29.29	82	2½ L	1/200 F
31.7	Hitchin	32.49	76/81	2¾ L	1/200 F
37	Arlesey	36.38	78		1/200, 1/400 F
41.1	Biggleswade	39.49	78½		1/264 F
47.4	Tempsford	44.42	76		L
51.6	St Neots	48.04	74½		1/330 R
58.7	Huntingdon	53.41	78	1¼ E	L
63.4	Abbots Ripton	57.30	70		1/200 R
67	Connington South	60.10	81		1/200 F
69.1	Holme	61.47	76		L
		sigs/ sigs stand			
<u>76.3</u>	<u>Peterborough</u>	<u>75.34</u>	(69½ net)	5½ L	

The train left Peterborough on the slow line, but accelerated to 57mph by Tallington and then sustained 62mph through Little Bytham, falling to 59 at Corby Glen before a signal stand at Stoke summit. Grantham was passed at 77mph, and 6233 then topped 80 at Carlton, a minimum of 69 on the 1 in 200 to Dukeries Junction, and another 80 at Retford, before the Doncaster stop. The next high speed section was the impossibly timed 44.1 miles from York to Darlington, level or slightly against the grade, where 6233 sustained 75-78mph all the way, achieving a time of 40 minutes 13 seconds start-to-stop. The return journey was even more spectacular. Inspector Andy Taylor, supported by Fireman Graeme Bunker, was in charge from Darlington to York, the 44.1 miles taking exactly 40 minutes with 80mph reached just after Northallerton (15 miles), 86 at Thirsk, falling to 82, then rising again to 86mph at Tollerton. Driver Ron Smith took over at York, with the inspector still on board and after a (relatively) quiet run to Doncaster, roared up to 85mph before Newark, 70mph minimum on the 1 in 200 to Askham Tunnel and 66½ nearing Stoke summit when the train was checked and diverted to the slow line, even then reaching 78mph on the descent. The 76.6 miles from Doncaster to Peterborough were completed in 78 minutes 38 seconds (around 74 net). On the last leg 6233 maintained 62½mph on the long 1 in 200 through Hitchin to Stevenage, before a final dash beyond Potters Bar to the terminus. 360 miles of the two runs on that day were completed at an average of 73.7mph, the longest sustained high speed in preservation. Three start-to-stop sections were covered at better than a mile a minute at 60.6, 64 and 66.1mph.

It continued to run main line charter trains, still in LMS red livery (see Driver Bill Andrew's recollections in the previous chapter). On 6 March 2010, 6233 was rolled out in LMS lined black livery, which was retained during 2010, before a major overhaul, taking 6233 out of service for the 2011 season. On 3 March 2012 the now renumbered 46233 was displayed in BR standard green livery, as used by British Railways during the early 1950s, at the Midland Railway - Butterley, following a major overhaul and main line running recommenced using Tyseley as base. On 9 September 2018, the engine regained its original number 6233 and LMS Crimson Lake livery to mark its 80th birthday.

46233 *Duchess of Sutherland* at Preston with the Down *Midday Scot*, 18 May 1957. (R.H.G. Simpson/MLS Collection)

124 • THE LMS PRINCESS CORONATION PACIFICS, THE FINAL YEARS & PRESERVATION

Above: **46233 when** allocated to Edge Hill on the 2pm Liverpool Lime St – Euston at Minshull Vernon approaching Crewe, 27 February 1962. (MLS Collection)

Right: **6233** *Duchess of Sutherland* as restored in LMS red livery for Butlin's at the Heads of Ayr holiday camp and secured by the Bressingham Museum, c1973. (Author's Collection)

6233 *Duchess of Sutherland* with the 40th Anniversary of the *Caledonian's* last run special at Oubeck, en route to Carlisle, 4 September 2004. (John Shuttleworth)

46233 *Duchess of Sutherland* on test near Willington with a *Night Owl* charter special after overhaul at Butterley and restoration in late BR green livery, 29 March 2012. (John Hillier)

46235

6235 was built in June 1939 in streamlined form at a cost of £9,437 and was the first to be de-streamlined in April 1946. It was withdrawn from Crewe North shed, where it had spent its entire career, in September 1964 after running 1,566,677 miles. The engine after withdrawal came into Crewe Works for examination and repair before being restored for museum preservation, but according to Keith Collier, a Crewe fitter at the Works at the time, there was little wrong needing attention. 46235 was prepared by BR for preservation and painted in the BR green livery that it wore in the 1950s until its withdrawal. After storage at Nuneaton MPD it was moved in May 1966 to the Birmingham Museum of Science and Industry,

46235 *City of Birmingham* as de-streamlined in 1946, and retaining smoothed smokebox top, painted BR blue, and seen at Blackpool, 21 April 1951. (R.K. Blencowe/MLS Collections)

46235 *City of Birmingham* at Carlisle Kingmoor shed, 15 May 1960. (MLS Collection)

Above left: **46235** *City of Birmingham* passing Upperby having taken over the 9.56am Glasgow-Euston after the failure of 70000 at Carlisle, 13 June 1964. (A.C. Gilbert/MLS Collection)

Above right: **46235 in** the paint shop at Crewe Works being prepared for the Birmingham Museum of Science & Industry, 27 March 1966. (MLS Collection)

Above left: **46235** *City of Birmingham* as presented by British Railways to the Birmingham Museum of Science & Industry, 1964. (Real Photographs/MLS Collection)

Above right: **46235** *City of Birmingham* as displayed at the Birmingham Museum, 22 October 1966. (W. Potter/MLS Collection)

which was built around the locomotive. It was placed on a short length of track and could be moved by hydraulic rams for a few feet so that its motion in operation could be viewed. After closure of that museum, 46235 was moved into the new Birmingham Museum of Science and Discovery in 2001. Unlike the other two surviving members of the class, *City of Birmingham* has never steamed in preservation.

Chapter 7
CONCLUSIONS

How might the 'Princess Coronation' locomotives have been further developed? In the 1930s, very significant developments were taking place in France with André Chapelon's rebuilding of a Paris-Orleans compound pacific with generous streamlined internal steam passages and Kylchap exhaust. At the end of the Second World War, Chapelon had developed his ideas and built a mighty three-cylinder 4-8-4, 242 A 1, which could on test produce an incredible 5,500ihp. In America, the Pennsylvanian Railroad's two-cylinder simple K4S pacific with mechanical stoking and Kiesel star shaped blastpipe of 1914 was achieving a prodigious power output equalling the French pacific and one modified with Franklin poppet valves reached 4,200ihp. Like the French, mightier 4-6-4s existed such as the New York Railroad 'Hudsons' and the same railroad's post-war 4-8-4 'Niagaras', the latter being capable of well over 6,000ihp. And similarly, the 1941 class J 4-8-4s of the Norfolk & Western, the 1937 Union Pacific Railroad FEF-3 4-8-4s and the 1937 GS 4-8-4s of the Southern Pacific were massive and performing prodigious feats of haulage on express passenger services.

However, the British loading gauge stymied the development of the Stanier pacific on either of these lines. The German high speed '05' 4-6-4 was restricted to 160kph (100mph) in normal traffic and the 3-cylinder 1939 streamlined pacifics were no more powerful and more prone to failure than the Stanier engines until their rebuilding as non-streamlined oil-burning pacifics as the 01.10 (012) class in the mid-1950s. The culmination of German pacific design with the two Krupp 3-cylinder Class 10s in 1956, whilst theoretically more powerful, failed to achieve their potential and had a poor reliability and availability record.

A 4-6-4 development of the Princess Coronation in streamlined form had been mooted in 1939 and drawings (see appendix page 169) were resurrected by Tom Coleman and Ernest Cox in 1942 as an authorised order of Stanier pacifics was still outstanding, but in the war years such further development was not appropriate and as the shortage of powerful pacifics for the heavy wartime traffic became more acute, more Stanier pacifics, both streamlined and non-streamlined, were built in conventional form in 1943/4. An ambitious 4-8-4 non-streamlined locomotive was also proposed, but this was for heavy freight work with 5ft 6in coupled wheels. However, the LMS 8F design was in mass production at Swindon, Brighton and Doncaster as well as Crewe and development of a fast freight design would have to wait until Riddles' 9F 2-10-0.

The next step to develop the Stanier pacific was H.G. Ivatt's 46256 and 46257 in 1947/8, but the changes here were to improve mileage between repairs and availability in post-war conditions rather than any increase in either power or speed performance. Then the opportunity came in 1950 with debate about the future of the LMS Turbomotive, 46202. A recommendation was made to the Railway Executive in April 1951 to convert it to a 4-cylinder reciprocating conventional pacific at a cost of £6,250 and this was approved. The conversion took place over three months in 1952, costing in reality £8,774, and involved a new front end to the frame to allow the 4-cylinder layout and 'Duchess' style motion arrangement but the retention of 6ft 6in wheels of the Princess Royal design and a boiler from that class (previously on 46204) but with an increased superheat of 720 sq ft. The rebuilt 46202 was put into traffic in August 1952, named *Princess Anne,* and was allocated to regular

Euston-Liverpool runs where it is said to have performed in a similar fashion to the other pacifics though no exceptional logs have surfaced during its short two-month career before it was involved in the catastrophic triple train accident at Harrow and Wealdstone in October 1952.

The next development is controversial. The 'Jubilee' pilot engine to 46202 involved in the accident, 45637, was severely damaged and scrapped, but both the remains of 46202 and 46242, the engine of the Up Perth train that caused the crash, were removed to Crewe and examined to consider repair. Although 46202 appeared to be less damaged than 46242, the latter was repaired at a cost of some £7-8,000 and 46202 was scrapped despite a similar estimate for repair, although many of its parts were repaired and reused on other engines. In fact, the intact front end of 46202's frame was cut and welded to the back end of 46242's frame, the boiler was repaired and set on 46212's frame and the tender (No.9003) which was hardly damaged was attached to 8F 48134 for the rest of that engine's life. There is a strong case to suggest that 46202's withdrawal was an excuse to develop a new 8P locomotive that would make a significant advance on the Stanier Duchess. 71000 *Duke of Gloucester* was Riddles' last attempt to demonstrate that steam power still had a place in a modernised railway, but it cost nearly £45,000 to build, some £35,000 more than the repair of 46202 would have done. The Caprotti valve gear and cylinder efficiency was excellent but other design failings meant that 71000 was a disappointment and it never in BR days matched the consistent performance of the Duchesses. Time for steam was running out and there was no serious attempt to identify and remedy its defects before widespread dieselisation and it was only in preservation and much attention by its new engineering team that the missed opportunities were revealed. However, Keith Collier, a former fitter from Crewe Works in the 1950s, became CME for the restoration of 71000, and stated that the principal problem with 71000 was its excessive harsh draught from the standard double chimney which caused high coal consumption and the fire to be thrown with loss of steaming capacity, when the right move would have been to provide it with a Kylchap exhaust system – rejected at the time, but provided in preservation and transforming its performance.

One last opportunity to move the Stanier pacific performance a step forward was the idea of equipping members of the class with a mechanical stoker so that the power of the locomotive could be fully utilised without requiring excessive effort from a single fireman or the cost of running with two. But that idea also came too late and further expenditure on steam was very limited once the Modernisation Plan of 1955 had been announced. Some useful investment was made on both the Eastern and Western regions with the provision of double chimneys for the A3s, Kings and Castles and the Southern substantially rebuilt the Merchant Navies and a majority of the Bulleid light pacifics, but that was essentially a cost cutting exercise to improve reliability, availability and fuel costs without impairing performance.

So how did the Duchess pacifics compare with their contemporaries in the UK? Reading through the conclusions of other authors and listening to drivers, firemen and fitters who had experience of them, coupled with my own observations from the mid-1950s for the following ten years, I suggest that they were undoubtedly the most powerful of Britain's express locomotives although they were not able to consistently fulfil their full potential. They could run fast, not only in their streamlined form, but the occasions when they could demonstrate their 100mph capability were rare as their West Coast main line home track had few long straight stretches like the descent from Stoke on the GN main line or down from Badminton through Hullavington on the Western. The steep descents from Grayrigg, Shap and Beattock had curvature that limited speeds and logs on these downhill sections usually showed frequent touching of the brake. There is the possibility – even the probability – that one could have matched the German '05' or Gresley A4 at 120mph or more given a suitable length of good track, but the opportunity did not arise. Therefore, the Gresley A4 stands supreme as the UK's fastest locomotive, not just for its one-off record, but the frequency with which it reached 90-100mph speeds on regular East Coast expresses, both pre- and post-war.

The Stanier pacific's mastery over the northern fell banks of Grayrigg and Shap and the Scottish Beattock probably surpassed the ability of any other UK locomotive on a regular and consistent basis, but its liability to slip badly in wet or misty conditions was a drawback that sometimes prevented the full use of the power available. Indeed, some drivers preferred the 'Princess Royals' on the northern banks as with 6ft 6in coupled wheels they were more reliable in holding their feet on both starting and on the banks, especially if checked at awkward places like Scout Green or Harthope. This was even more the case when compared with the performance of the Great Western 'Kings' over the short but steep banks of South Devon. The few opportunities for the Duchesses there have shown both their remarkable power when conditions were right and equally their frailty on damp rails. The 4-6-0 wheel arrangement and increased adhesion of the 'King' undoubtedly was an advantage there. Keith Collier with his preservation experience of 71000 believes that had the Ivatt pair been equipped with coil springs to the rear truck instead of the Delta or Bissel truck, much of the adhesion problem would have been overcome and would then have caused similar modification to the rest of the class. In his personal view and experience in the everyday world of reality the 'Princess Royal' was the better locomotive. It was a better starter with its six foot six inch drivers, four separate sets of valve gear, and equal length con rods. It was his belief that the 'Princess Royals' should have been updated instead of new build Duchesses by fitting them with a shortened boiler with 5½in flues with a decent A/S ratio, a Kylchap type front end with a double chimney, Goodfellow blast pipe tips, roller bearings, a long travel coiled sprung Delta truck, bigger piston valves, and higher superheat.

But in my view and that of most of the drivers who worked them on long non-stop runs with heavy loads, especially the night sleepers from London and Birmingham to Glasgow and Perth, they had no equals. Perhaps only the Peppercorn A1s and A2s might have matched them on such duties, although they too could come to grief with excessive slipping on occasions. Three A1s were loaned to Polmadie in the early 1950s but they did not make much impact. The Duchesses were undoubtedly superb engines but their full potential in my opinion was never reached consistently in traffic, marred too often by slow schedules and indifferent LMR operating on the congested West Coast route, that was affected by electrification work from 1957 onwards.

The best BR class 8P ever? Maybe. On road tests with 6234 in 1939, on the Rugby Test Plant and Settle & Carlisle line with 46225 in 1955 and with the experience of 46229 and 46233 in the preservation era, their superiority

Chapelon's first rebuild of a Paris-Orleans pacific, 3566, at Tours, November 1929. Later rebuilds of the P-O machines and new constructions in the late 1930s became SNCF class 231 E which were used on the Nord Region until the mid-1960s. Maximum speed in service 130kph (81mph), 174kph (108.75mph) on test. (SNCF official photograph/MLS Collection)

was demonstrated, but in normal traffic conditions in the 1950s before dieselisation? Flashes of brilliance and successful haulage of heavy trains, especially overnight. Let me put it this way – I can't see any other BR 8P locomotive improving on their performance had they been on the West Coast main line in place of the Stanier Duchesses. And most others would have struggled to match them.

Chapelon's prototype 4-8-4 'super' express locomotive, 3-cylinder compound 242 A 1, rebuilt between 1943 and 1946 from Etat 4-8-2 241-101, seen here on a postcard, 1950. It reached 5,500ihp and 158kph (99mph) on test. It remained unique because of the SNCF electrification policy and was withdrawn and scrapped in 1960. (MLS Collection)

Pennsylvania Railroad 2-cylinder K4S pacific, No.1361, built in 1918, tractive effort 44,460lb, 90mph max, 3,286ihp. 425 were built between 1914 and 1927, the last being withdrawn in 1960. It is seen at Monmouth Park Racetrack, Oceanport, New Jersey, 6 July 1954. This locomotive is now one of two of the class preserved. (Robert F. Collins/MLS Collection)

132 • THE LMS PRINCESS CORONATION PACIFICS, THE FINAL YEARS & PRESERVATION

Above left: **Pennsylvania Railroad** 2-cylinder K4S pacific, 3768, one of ten streamlined, built in 1920 and withdrawn in 1960. (Author's Collection)

Above right: **New York** Central Railroad's 'Hudson' 4-6-4, No.5436, built in 1937. 275 were built between 1927 and 1938. Tractive effort was 41,860lbs and max speed 110mph. They were fitted with boosters to aid starting, but they were primarily used on level high speed routes. (Author's Collection)

New York Central Railroad's 'Hudson' J-3a 4-6-4, No.5424, departing from Collinwood Ohio, for Buffalo, New York State, August 1949. (William W. Rinn/MLS Collection)

Above: **New York** Central Railroad's 'Hudson' 4-6-4, No.5453, one of the last ten classified J-3, built in 1938, and streamlined. (Author's Collection)

Below left: **New York** Central Railroad's 'Niagara' 4-8-4, No.6001 built in 1945, 25 in total by 1946. They had two massive cylinders, 25½ in x 32 in. Power output calculated at 6,680hp at 85mph, over 6,000hp achieved on tests in comparison with diesels, tractive effort 62,333lbs. The class was made redundant by rapid dieselisation and all were withdrawn by 1956. (Author's Collection)

Below right: **New York** Central Railroad's 'Niagara' 4-8-4, No.6024 ready to depart from Detroit, Michigan, May 1946. 6024 completed 288,849 miles between New York & Chicago in one 11-month period. (Ed Nowak/MLS Collection)

Above left: **Preserved Union** Pacific's FEF-3 4-8-4, No.8444 on a US National Railway Historical Society special from Denver to Sterling at La Salle, 16 July 1982. This engine, then numbered 844, was the last of 45 engines built between 1937 and 1944. It was an oil-burner with two 25in x 32in cylinders and 300lb psi boiler, tractive effort 63,800lb, and was capable of 120mph and hauling 1,000 ton trains on level track at 100mph. It is based since preservation in Cheyenne, Wyoming. (A.C. Gilbert/MLS Collections)

Above right: **Norfolk &** Western Railroad 4-8-4 of class J built in 1941, No.600 heads the streamliner *The Tennessean* west of Roanoke, Virginia, c1942. It was a 27in x 32in 2-cylinder engine, with 300lb psi boiler pressure, and 5ft 10in driving wheels, tractive effort 80,000lbs, and is recorded to have timed a 1,025 ton train at 110mph on level track. (Norfolk & Western RR official photograph/MLS Collection)

The German Reichsbahn record-breaking locomotive, 4-6-4 05.002 being prepared for a test run at Hamburg Altona depot, April 1936. It achieved 200.4kph (125mph) between Hamburg and Berlin on a test run on 11 May 1936 but was then stopped for a week to retube the boiler. (Walter Höllnagel/Eisenbahnstiftung Collection)

Conclusions • 135

Above left: **Preserved DB** 3-cylinder oil-burning 01.10 pacific, 01.1100, built in 1940, de-streamlined in 1949, converted to oil firing in 1956 and withdrawn in 1975. It was subsequently preserved and is seen here on a rail enthusiasts' special at Altenbeken in 1995. (David Maidment)

Above right: **DB 3-cylinder** oil-burning pacific 10.001 built by Krupp in 1956, seen here at Braunschweig (Brunswick) Works, shortly before withdrawal and preservation, 24 August 1967. (MLS Collection)

Below: **The 1947** H.G. Ivatt version of the Stanier Duchess, 46256 *Sir William Stanier FRS* at Crewe South shed the day after it had operated its last special RCTS charter train, 27 September 1964. It was withdrawn from traffic, the last of its class, a week later. (A.C. Gilbert/MLS Collection)

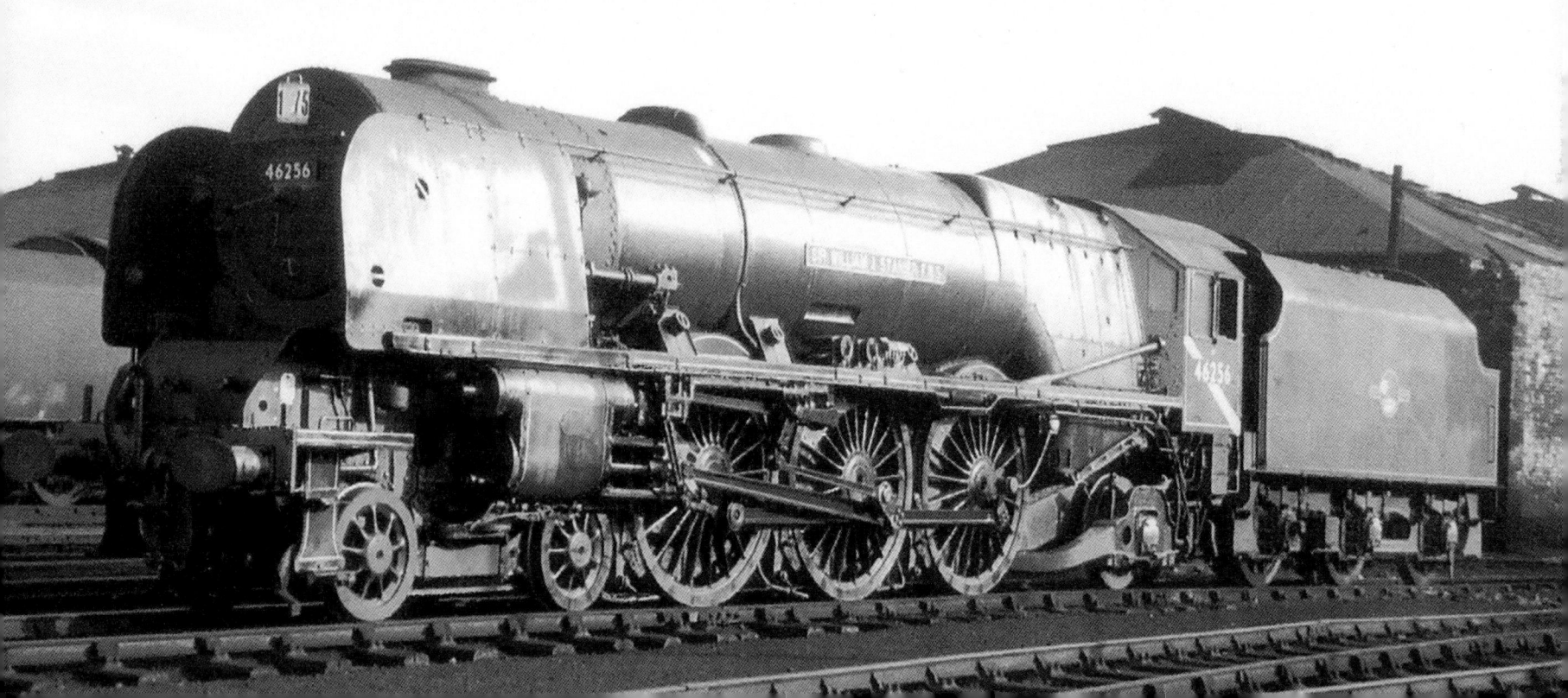

136 • THE LMS PRINCESS CORONATION PACIFICS, THE FINAL YEARS & PRESERVATION

Above: **Turbomotive 46202** after its last overhaul in that form at Crewe, 1950. (MLS Collection)

Right: **Rebuilt Turbomotive** 46202 *Princess Anne* departing from Crewe with the 7.50am to Euston a month before its destruction in the Harrow & Wealdstone train crash, September 1952. (MLS Collection)

Below left: **71000 Duke** *of Gloucester* as built in 1954. (MLS Collection)

Below right: **71000 Duke** *of Gloucester* leaving Shrewsbury for Crewe with a stopping train, running in after overhaul at Crewe Works, c1956. (MLS Collection)

COLOUR SECTION

A selection of colour prints and slides was made available from the archive of the Manchester Locomotive Society, nearly all from collections of former members and donated to the society. Most are from 1960 or after.

46245 *City of London* at the head of the Down *Caledonian*, Summer 1957. (Colour Rail)

Changing engines at Carlisle on the *Royal Scot* from Camden's 46240 *City of Coventry* to Polmadie's 46221 *Queen Elizabeth,* c1957.
(Colour Rail)

46232 *Duchess of Montrose* after repainting during its 1958 overhaul, at Crewe Works Yard.
(MLS Collection)

Colour Section • 139

Carlisle Upperby's 46220 *Coronation* on arrival at Euston after arriving with an overnight sleeper service, c1960. (MLS Collection)

46254 City of Stoke on Trent, recently ex-works, returned to its home depot of Crewe North, c1958. (J.R.Carter/MLS Collection)

140 • THE LMS PRINCESS CORONATION PACIFICS, THE FINAL YEARS & PRESERVATION

46225 Duchess of Gloucester rests on Carlisle Upperby shed, 1963. (MLS Collection)

Two Duchess pacifics, 46245 City of London and 46240 City of Coventry rest in the darkness of Camden shed shortly before its closure in 1963. (MLS Collection)

Colour Section • 141

Upperby's 46226 *Duchess of Norfolk* waits to attach a coach to a Glasgow-Euston express at Carlisle Citadel station, 27 May 1959. (R.C. Riley)

46226 *Duchess of Norfolk* at Shap Wells with the 9.15am Euston-Perth & Aberdeen, 25 June 1960. (A.C. Gilbert/MLS Collection)

142 • THE LMS PRINCESS CORONATION PACIFICS, THE FINAL YEARS & PRESERVATION

Polmadie's 46227 *Duchess of Devonshire* with steam to spare on the climb to Shap summit with an Anglo-Scottish express including two LNER Gresley and a Thompson coach at the head of the train, c1960. (MLS Collection)

46247 *City of Liverpool* tackles the climb to Beattock Summit easily with the 8-coach *Royal Scot*, c1959. (MLS Collection)

Colour Section • 143

Camden's 46229 *Duchess of Hamilton* with the Stranraer boat train, *The Shamrock*, near Bourne End, c1958. (MLS Collection)

Crewe North's 46225 *Duchess of Gloucester* climbs away from Lancaster with a Glasgow – Birmingham express, c1958. (MLS Collection)

144 • THE LMS PRINCESS CORONATION PACIFICS, THE FINAL YEARS & PRESERVATION

Camden's 46239 *City of Chester* with a Manchester – Euston express near Colwich, Cannock Chase in the background, c1960. (MLS Collection)

46241 *City of Edinburgh* of Crewe North depot leaves Lancaster with a Glasgow – Birmingham express, c1959. (MLS Collection)

46238 *City of Carlisle* passes Scout Green Box on its climb to Shap Summit with a relief Euston – Glasgow express, c1962. (MLS Collection)

Carlisle Upperby's 46255 *City of Hereford* has replaced the booked Camden Duchess on the 3.45pm Euston – Glasgow *Caledonian* and is seen departing Euston, 3 May 1960. (MLS Collection)

146 • THE LMS PRINCESS CORONATION PACIFICS, THE FINAL YEARS & PRESERVATION

Carlisle Kingmoor's 46244 *King George VI* takes water at Carstairs on a southbound relief express, c1962. (MLS Collection)

46254 *City of Stoke-on-Trent* picking up water from Dillicar troughs with the Up *Royal Scot*, c1958. (MLS Collection)

Polmadie's 46230 *Duchess of Buccleuch* picking up water from Dillicar troughs in the Lune Valley with an 8-coach Glasgow-London relief train, August 1960. (Derek Cross)

Polmadie's 46223 *Princess Alice* with a Glasgow-Carlisle train via the G&SWR route at Polquhap near New Cumnock, c1960. (Derek Cross)

148 • THE LMS PRINCESS CORONATION PACIFICS, THE FINAL YEARS & PRESERVATION

46227 *Duchess of Devonshire* descending Beattock bank, near Harthope, with a Glasgow-Euston express, c1961. (MLS Collection)

46228 *Duchess of Rutland* with a Down express passing Lichfield station, c1961. (MLS Collection)

Carlisle Kingmoor's 46244 *King George VI* tops Beattock Summit with steam to spare on a Euston – Glasgow relief train, c1962. (MLS Collection)

Camden's 46245 *City of London* on the Penrith/Keswick portion of *The Lakes Express* sails up Shap Bank, Summer 1963. (MLS Collection)

150 • THE LMS PRINCESS CORONATION PACIFICS, THE FINAL YEARS & PRESERVATION

46246 *City of Manchester* makes a dramatic exit from Euston station climbing Camden bank, with an early morning departure, 1961. (MLS Collection)

A few months later 46246 *City of Manchester* is stored out of use at Camden. It was never used again and was withdrawn and scrapped at Crewe Works in January 1963, the first English based Duchess to be withdrawn. (MLS Collection)

Colour Section • 151

46251 *City of Nottingham* passing over Moore troughs with the 11am Birmingham-Glasgow express, 4 August 1961. (A.C. Gilbert/MLS Collection)

A heavy Glasgow-Birmingham express at Lamington with 'Black 5' 45082 assisting Polmadie's 46230 *Duchess of Buccleuch,* September 1961. A Great Western coach for detaching at Crewe for the West of England is at the front. (Derek Cross)

152 • THE LMS PRINCESS CORONATION PACIFICS, THE FINAL YEARS & PRESERVATION

Upperby's 46238 *City of Carlisle* picking up water on Dillicar troughs in the Lune Valley with a relief Euston-Glasgow express, 13 July 1963. (A.C. Gilbert/MLS Collection)

Polmadie's 46242 *City of Glasgow* at Carlisle Kingmoor shed, 16 June 1963. Note the curved running plate to the front bufferbeam as restored after 46242's rebuilding after the Harrow & Wealdstone accident. (A.C. Gilbert/MLS Collection)

Colour Section • 153

46245 *City of London* at Greenholme with a relief London-Glasgow express, c1963. (MLS Collection)

46248 *City of Leeds* restarts a Wolverhampton-Euston express from Birmingham New Street with a thunderous slip, c1963. (Tony Waterfield/MLS Collection)

154 • THE LMS PRINCESS CORONATION PACIFICS, THE FINAL YEARS & PRESERVATION

Upperby's 46237 *City of Bristol* with withdrawn 46200 *The Princess Royal* and an LMS 2P 4-4-0, at Carlisle Upperby shed, 30 August 1964. (N. Fields/MLS Collection)

On a dull day a month later 46238 *City of Carlisle* has been cleaned up for standby Royal Train duties, Carlisle Upperby shed, 13 June 1964. (A.C. Gilbert/MLS Collection)

46225 *Duchess of Gloucester* restarts from a signal check at Winwick Junction with a down freight, Summer 1964. (MLS Collection)

Carlisle Upperby's 46250 *City of Lichfield* climbing the bank out of Lancaster with an Up parcels train, November 1963. (MLS Collection)

156 • THE LMS PRINCESS CORONATION PACIFICS, THE FINAL YEARS & PRESERVATION

46238 *City of Carlisle* relegated to fitted freight duties at Greenholme in the summer of 1964.
(MLS Collection)

Carlisle Kingmoor's 46244 *King George VI* departing from Perth with a fish train for Billingsgate Market, 1963.
(MLS Collection)

Colour Section • 157

46225 *Duchess of Gloucester* toils up Shap with a northbound freight, being banked at the rear, 1964.
(MLS Collection)

46256 *Sir William A. Stanier FRS* draws away from Carnforth with a northbound parcels train, Summer 1964.
(MLS Collection)

158 • THE LMS PRINCESS CORONATION PACIFICS, THE FINAL YEARS & PRESERVATION

46238 *City of Carlisle* standing on Holyhead shed alongside 'Black 5' 44770, August 1964.
(A.C. Gilbert/MLS Collection)

46238 *City of Carlisle* departing from Holyhead Harbour station with a train for Crewe and Euston, August 1964.
(A.C. Gilbert/MLS Collection)

Colour Section • 159

46240 *City of Coventry* at Willesden shed, prepared for a special working, 8 March 1964.
(W. Potter/MLS Collection)

46240 *City of Coventry* now with yellow stripe on cabside, at Willesden depot, August 1964.
(A.P. Downley/MLS Collection)

160 • THE LMS PRINCESS CORONATION PACIFICS, THE FINAL YEARS & PRESERVATION

46256 *Sir William Stanier FRS* leading 'Black 5' 45434 on a Down parcels train through Nuneaton station, 1964.
(MLS Collection)

46256 *Sir William Stanier FRS* at Carlisle Citadel station after arriving with the RCTS charter last Duchess trip, 26 September 1964.
(N. Fields/MLS Collection)

Colour Section • 161

46251 *City of Nottingam* at Edinburgh Princes Street with a return RCTS charter train to Crewe, 5 October 1963. (A.C.Gilbert/MLS Collection)

46251 *City of Nottingham* at Swindon shed after working an RCTS railtour to the Works. Alongside is 7022 *Hereford Castle*, standby that day to the Ian Allan 'Castle' high speed railtour to Plymouth returning via Bristol, 9 May 1964. (MLS Collection)

162 • THE LMS PRINCESS CORONATION PACIFICS, THE FINAL YEARS & PRESERVATION

46250 *City of Lichfield* at its home depot, Carlisle Upperby, standing by to cover any locomotive failures, summer 1964
(MLS Collection)

46245 *City of London* at Crewe with the return leg of the Ian Allan railtour from Paddington, 1 September 1964.
(MLS Collection)

46245 *City of London*, formerly of Camden, at Willesden after that depot's closure, 1964. (MLS Collection)

Driver Bill Andrew backing 6233 *Duchess of Sutherland* onto a charter train at Crewe. (Phil Matthews/Bill Andrew Collection)

After alteration to the smokebox 6229 was repainted in the LMS 1946 lined black livery on one side of the locomotive only for a few days for photographers, and then it was given its BR number and the lion and wheel decal on the tender, a livery only borne by 46247 *City of Liverpool* between December 1952 and February 1954. It is seen here at Tyseley in the Spring of 2006. (Bob Meanley)

The preserved 6233 *Duchess of Sutherland* in LMS black livery, passing Doncaster on a York – Kings Cross raitour, 17 May 2010 (Bill Andrew Collection)

The streamlined 6229 *Duchess of Hamilton* en route from Tyseley to the National Railway Museum at York, accompanied by Bob Meanley seen here in the cab, May 2009 (Bob Meanley Collection)

166 • THE LMS PRINCESS CORONATION PACIFICS, THE FINAL YEARS & PRESERVATION

The Hornby model of streamlined 6225 *Duchess of Gloucester* presented to the author at the annual 'Crewe Dinner' in London when he substituted at short notice for Boris Johnson in giving the after dinner speech. (David Maidment)

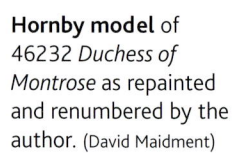

Hornby model of 46232 *Duchess of Montrose* as repainted and renumbered by the author. (David Maidment)

Colour Section • 167

The author's model of 46244 *King George VI* 'crownlined' and repainted by a Maidenhead model shop craftsman in the 1980s. (David Maidment)

The most recent 2020 Hornby model of 46257 *City of Salford* as purchased out of the box. (David Maidment)

Three styles of 'Princess Coronation' nameplates as first used on the streamlined engines in 1937, 6224 *Princess Alexandra*, 6221 *Queen Elizabeth* and 6222 *Queen Mary*, on display at the National Railway Museum, 10 December 2021. (David Maidment)

APPENDIX

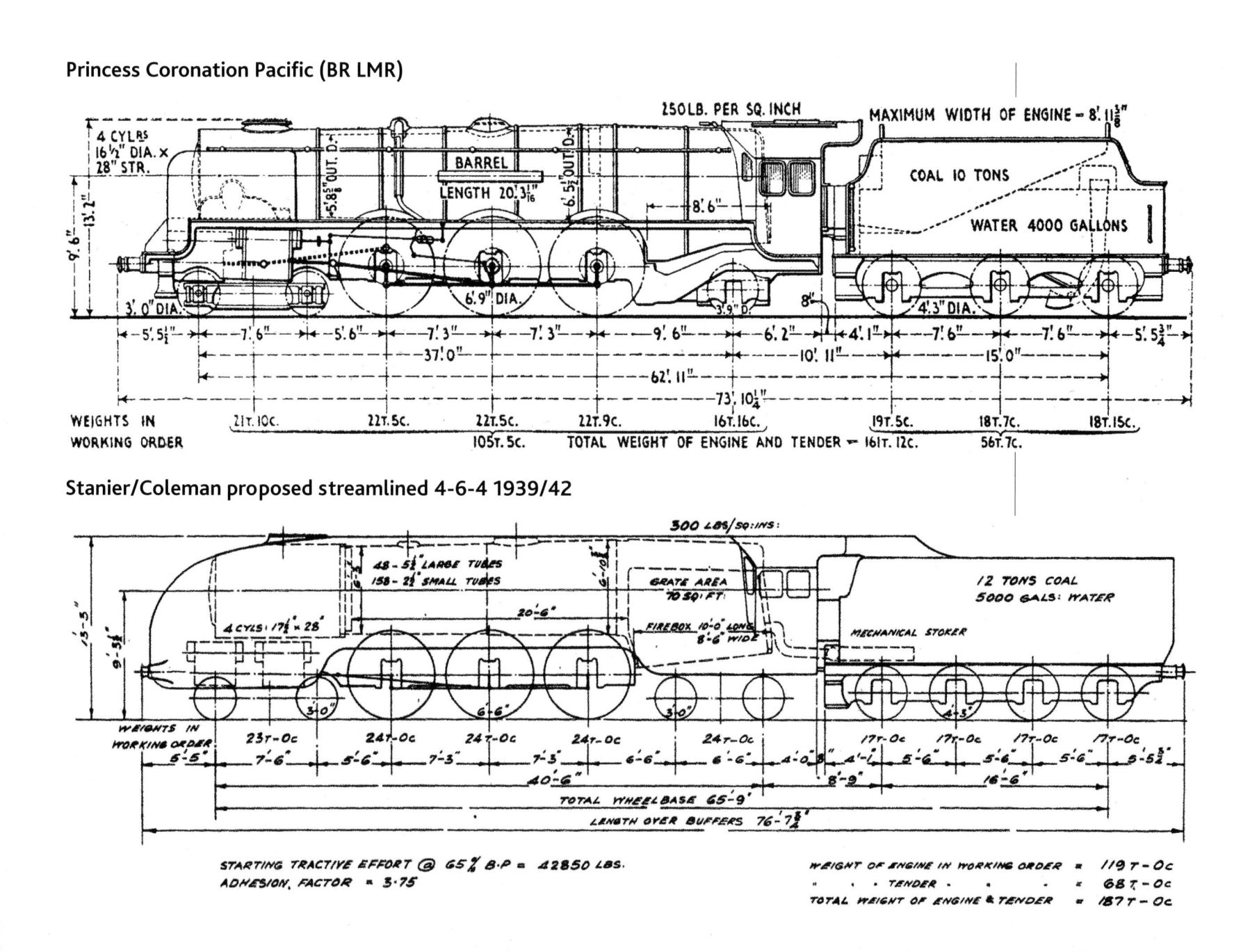

Princess Coronation Pacific (BR LMR)

Stanier/Coleman proposed streamlined 4-6-4 1939/42

Rebuilt Turbomotive 46202 1952

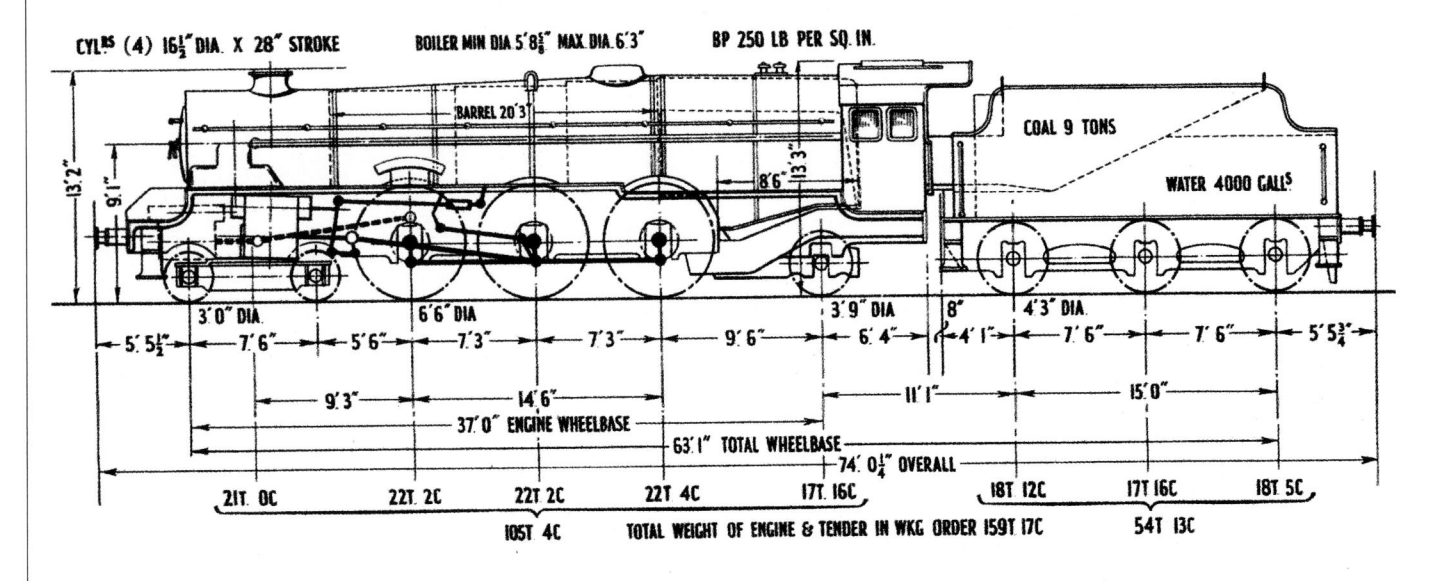

Statistics

No.	Name	Built	De-streamlined	D/chimney	Withdrawn	Mileage
46220	*Coronation*	6/37	11/46	12/44	4/63	1,527,266
46221	*Queen Elizabeth*	6/37	5/46	11/40	5/63	1,512,212
46222	*Queen Mary*	6/37	5/46	8/43	10/63	1,448,790
46223	*Princess Alice*	7/37	8/46	11/41	10/63	1,461,772
46224	*Princess Alexandra*	7/37	5/46	5/40	10/63	1,402,275
46225	*Duchess of Gloucester*	5/38	2/47	6/43	9/64	1,742,642
46226	*Duchess of Norfolk*	5/38	6/47	7/42	9/64	1,423,044
46227	*Duchess of Devonshire*	6/38	2/47	12/40	12/62	1,210,818
46228	*Duchess of Rutland*	6/38	7/47	9/40	9/64	1,428,042
46229	*Duchess of Hamilton*	9/38	11/47	4/43	2/64	1,533,846 Preserved
46230	*Duchess of Buccleuch*	6/38	-	10/40	11/63	1,255,044
46231	*Duchess of Atholl*	6/38	-	6/40	12/62	1,262,100
46232	*Duchess of Montrose*	7/38	-	1/43	12/62	1,217,958
46233	*Duchess of Sutherland*	7/38	-	3/41	2/64	1,657,270 Preserved
46234	*Duchess of Abercorn*	8/38	-	2/39	1/63	1,463,238
46235	*City of Birmingham*	7/39	4/46	New	9/64	1,566,677 Preserved
46236	*City of Bradford*	7/39	12/47	New	9/64	1,332,840
46237	*City of Bristol*	8/39	1/47	New	9/64	1,448,740

Appendix

No.	Name	Built	De-streamlined	D/chimney	Withdrawn	Mileage
46238	*City of Carlisle*	9/39	11/46	New	9/64	1,319,020
46239	*City of Chester*	9/39	6/47	New	9/64	1,525,120
46240	*City of Coventry*	3/40	6/47	New	9/64	1,348,031
46241	*City of Edinburgh*	4/40	1/47	New	9/64	1,371,838
46242	*City of Glasgow*	5/40	3/47	New	10/63	1,307,542
46243	*City of Lancaster*	6/40	5/49	New	9/64	1,231,390
46244	*King George VI*	7/40	8/47	New	9/64	1,358,405
46245	*City of London*	6/43	8/47	New	9/64	1,103,488
46246	*City of Manchester*	8/43	9/46	New	1/63	1,140,096
46247	*City of Liverpool*	9/43	5/47	New	5/63	1,129,184
46248	*City of Leeds*	10/43	12/46	New	9/64	1,119,104
46249	*City of Sheffield*	4/44	-	New	11/63	1,047,855
46250	*City of Lichfield*	5/44	-	New	9/64	1,035,855
46251	*City of Nottingham*	6/44	-	New	9/64	948,750
46252	*City of Leicester*	6/44	-	New	5/63	975,975
46253	*City of St Albans*	9/46	-	New	5/63	911,391
46254	*City of Stoke-on-Trent*	9/46	-	New	9/64	828,880
46255	*City of Hereford*	10/46	-	New	9/64	824,174
46256	*Sir William Stanier FRS*	12/47	-	New	10/64	762,048
46257	*City of Salford*	2/48	-	New	9/64	765,028

Livery Changes

No.	BR number	Blue	Red	Plain black	Lined black	BR blue	BR Green	BR red
46220	7/48	6/37	-	3/44	11/46	1/50	8/52	-
46221	10/48	6/37	11/40	-	6/46	3/50	12/52	-
46222	9/48	6/37	-	8/44	5/46	10/50	12/53	-
46223	3/49	7/37	-	1/44	8/46	4/50	10/52	-
46224	5/48	7/37	-	8/44	6/46	5/48*, 8/50	5/52	-
46225	6/48	-	5/38	8/44	3/47	3/50	1/55	8/58 **
46226	9/48	-	5/38	5/44	6/47, 9/48++	6/51	5/54	11/58 **
46227	5/48	-	6/38	12/43	8/46	4/50	10/52	-
46228	7/48	-	6/38	5/44	10/47	10/50	6/55	6/58***
46229	7/48	-	9/38	8/43	1/48	2/50	4/52	9/58 **
46230	5/48	-	6/38	-	9/46	5/48*	5/52	-

No.	BR number	Blue	Red	Plain black	Lined black	BR blue	BR Green	BR red
46231	5/48	-	6/38	9/45	8/46	1/51	12/53	-
46232	5/48	-	7/38	2/45	3/48	5/48*	11/51	-
46233	10/48	-	7/38	-	10/47	5/50	11/52	-
46234	10/48	-	8/38	+	10/48	-	2/52	-
46235	5/48	-	7/39	7/44	4/46#, 1/47	12/50	5/53	-
46236	4/48	-	7/39	4/44, 8/52	2/48	-	11/54	7/58 **
46237	7/48	-	8/39	8/44	3/47	9/49	3/55	-
46238	3/49	-	9/39	-/43	1/47, 3/49++	-	3/52	6/58***
46239	8/48	-	9/39	3/44	9/47	7/50	8/54	-
46240	6/48	-	3/40	12/44	7/47	1/50	10/54	7/58**
46241	5/48	-	4/40	5/43	2/47	5/48*, 9/49	6/53	-
46242	5/48	-	5/40	5/44	5/47	7/49	10/53	-
46243	4/48	-	6/40	12/43	-	6/49	2/54	10/58**
46244	8/48	-	7/40	1/44	9/47	10/50	7/53	10/58**
46245	8/48	-	-	6/43	10/47	-	4/53	12/57***
46246	11/48	-	-	8/43	10/46, 11/48++	-	6/53	10/58**
46247	11/48	-	-	9/43	6/47	-	2/54	5/58****
46248	3/49	-	-	10/43	12/46, 3/49++	-	1/53	6/58***
46249	4/48	-	-	4/44	11/47	9/50	10/54	-
46250	2/49	-	-	5/44	9/47	5/50	10/52	-
46251	5/48	-	-	6/44	8/47, 5/49++	-	2/55	11/58**
46252	4/49	-	-	6/44	7/49++	-	1/52	-
46253	9/49	-	-	-	9/46	-	11/53	-
46254	7/49	-	-	-	9/46	2/50	10/55	9/58**
46255	6/49	-	-	-	10/46	8/50	1/53	-
46256	5/48	-	-	-	12/47, 10/48++	5/51	6/54	5/58***
46257	New	-	-	-	5/48	-	10/52	-

  *   BR experimental dark blue
  ** BR red with BR lining initially, changed to LMS lining 1959/60
 *** BR red with LMS lining
**** BR red with LMS, then BR, then LMS lining again
 +   LMS experimental blue/grey, 3/46
 ++ BR lined black
 #   LMS unlined black

Allocations 1958 – withdrawal
Camden (1B), Crewe N (5A), Edge Hill (8A), Carlisle Upperby (12B), Carlisle Kingmoor (12A), Polmadie (66A)

No.	1958	1960	Final
46220	5A	5A	12B
46221	5A	5A	12B
46222	66A	66A	66A
46223	66A	66A	66A
46224	66A	66A	66A
46225	5A	12B	12B
46226	12B	12B	12A
46227	66A	66A	66A
46228	5A	5A	5A
46229	5A	5A	5A
46230	66A	66A	66A
46231	66A	66A	66A
46232	66A	66A	66A
46233	12B	8A	8A
46234	5A	12B	12B
46235	5A	5A	5A
46236	12B	12B	12A
46237	12B	12B	12B
46238	12B	12B	12B
46239	1B	1B	5A
46240	1B	1B	5A
46241	1B	5A	8A
46242	1B	1B	66A
46243	12B	1B	8A
46244	12B	12B	12A
46245	1B	1B	5A
46246	5A	1B	1B
46247	1B	1B	12A
46248	5A	5A	5A
46249	5A	5A	66A
46250	12B	12B	12B

No.	1958	1960	Final
46251	5A	5A	5A
46252	5A	12B	1B
46253	5A	5A	5A
46254	1B	5A	5A
46255	12B	12B	12A
46256	1B	5A	5A
46257	1B	12B	12A

Main Line Weekday Departures from Euston to Crewe & beyond, Summer Timetable 1960.

am
- 7.45 *Lancastrian* to Liverpool
- 8.00 *Irish Mail* to Holyhead
- 8.15 Liverpool & Manchester
- 9.05 *Royal Scot* to Glasgow
- 9.35 *Comet* to Manchester
- 9.50 Perth
- 10.00 Glasgow
- 10.10 *Manxman* to Liverpool
- 10.25 Barrow
- 10.35 Blackpool
- 11.15 Pwllheli
- 11.30 Manchester & Barrow
- 11.35 *Lakes Express* to Windermere

pm
- 12.05 *Red Rose* to Liverpool
- 1.05 *Midday Scot* to Glasgow
- 1.10 Perth
- 2.05 Liverpool
- 3.45 *Caledonian* to Glasgow
- 3.50 Manchester
- 4.20 Manchester
- 4.45 *Shamrock* to Liverpool
- 4.55 Blackpool
- 5.25 *Emerald Isle Express* to Holyhead
- 5.40 *Ulster Express* to Heysham
- 6.00 *Mancunian* to Manchester
- 6.10 *Merseyside Express* to Liverpool
- 6.30* *Royal Highlander* to Inverness
- 7.10* *Northern Irishman* to Stranraer
- 7.15* Oban & Perth
- 8.40* *Irish Mail* to Holyhead
- 8.50 Holyhead & Liverpool

9.00*   Motherwell & Glasgow
9.35*   Glasgow
10.30   Whitehaven
10.40* Perth
10.55* Windermere & Carlisle
11.40* Manchester & Glasgow

am
12.10* Glasgow
12.20* Liverpool

From Birmingham to Preston & beyond
am
7.10   Inverness
11.00   Glasgow
11.05   Edinburgh

pm
10.50* Glasgow & Edinburgh

* Sleeping car service

BIBLIOGRAPHY

Atkins, Philip, *William Stanier: The Man and his Locomotives*, article from *Fire- the Story of the End of Steam*, Steam Railway Publication, 1968.
Baker, Allan & Morrison, Gavin, *Crewe Sheds*, Ian Allan, 1988.
Becket, W.S., *The Xpress Locomotive Register, Vol. 2 – London Midland Region, 1950-1960*, Xpress Publishing, 1998.
Binns, Donald, *LMS Locomotives at Work – 2: 'Coronation' Class 4-6-2*, Wyvern Publications, 1988.
Blakemore, Michael & Rutherford, Michael, *Duchess of Hamilton, Ultimate in Pacific Power*, National Railway Museum, York, 1990.
Clay, John F., & Cliffe, J., *The West Coast Pacifics*, Ian Allan, 1976.
Cox, E.S., *World Steam in the Twentieth Century*, Ian Allan, 1969.
Doherty, Douglas, *The LMS Duchesses*, Model & Allied Publications Ltd., 1973.
Essery, Bob, & Jenkinson, David, *An Illustrated History of LMS Locomotives, Vol.5*, Silver Link Publications, 1989.
Ewart, Brell & Radford, Brian, *6233 Duchess of Sutherland and the Princess Coronation Class*, Princess Royal Locomotive Class Trust, 2002.
Hillier-Graves, Tim, *LMS Locomotive Design & Development, the Life & Work of Tom Coleman*, Pen & Sword, 2018
Hillier-Graves, Tim, *The Turbomotive Stanier's Advanced Pacific*, Pen & Sword, 2017.
Hunt, David, Jennison, John, Meanley, Bob, James, Fred, & Essery, Bob, *LMS Locomotive Profiles No.11 – The 'Coronation' Class Pacifics*, Wild Swan Publications, 2008.
Jenkinson, David, *The 'Coronation' Pacifics*, Railway World, April & May 1966.
Jenkinson, David, *The Power of the Duchesses*, Oxford Publishing Company, 1979.
Jenkinson, David, *Profile of the Duchesses*, Oxford Publishing Company, 1982.
Landau, D.H., *96 at Tring – with 46244*, article in *Trains Seventy One*, Ian Allan, 1970.
Maidment, David, *A Privileged Journey*, Pen & Sword, 2015.
Maidment, David, *An Indian Summer of Steam*, Pen & Sword, 2015.
Mannion, Roger J., *The Duchess, Stanier's Masterpiece*, Alan Sutton Publishing, 1996.
Meanley, Bob, 'A Supreme Effort' *Steam World Magazine* 500 and 'Earn Your Stripes', *Steam World* 501, December 2019 & January 2020 (the re-streamlining of 6229).
Nelson, Ronald I., *Locomotive Performance, A Footplate Survey*, Ian Allan, 1979.
Roundhouse Books, *LM Pacifics, A Pictorial Tribute*, Roundhouse Books, 1967.
Rowledge, J.W.P., *The L.M.S. Pacifics*, David & Charles, 1987.
Sixsmith, Ian, *The Book of the Coronation Pacifics*, Irwell Press, 1998.
Trains Illustrated, *Motive Power Miscellany LMR*, Ian Allan, January 1963 – December 1964.
Ward, D.H. & Bellwood, F.J., *The Restoration of Duchess of Hamilton*, Railway World, March 1981.

INDEX

Photographs
Location – Black & White
Acton Bridge, 41, 46
Ais Gill, 73
Altenbeken, Germany, 135
Ashton, 35
Balshaw Lane, 33
Bangor, 58, 65
Beattock station, 38
Beattock summit, 66
Betley Road, 36
Birmingham Museum of Science, 127
Blackpool, 126
Bletchley, 27
Blue Anchor, 115
Boars Head, 48
Bold Colliery Sidings, 116
Bressingham Museum, 124
Braunschweig (Brunswick) Germany, 135
Burnage, 25
Camden, 26, 43, 114
Carlisle Citadel, 30, 42-43, 47, 51-52, 73, 99
Carlisle Kingmoor, 11, 41, 126
Carlisle Upperby, 75-76, 127, 162
Carnforth, 67
Cheddington, 61
Chester, 63
Collinwood, Ohio, USA, 132
Crewe Heritage Centre, 101
Crewe North, 10, 72, 95-96
Crewe South, 63, 72-74, 135
Crewe station, 45, 59, 63, 77, 136
Crewe Works, 10, 114, 127, 136
Davenport Junction, 38

Detroit, Michigan, USA, 133
Dillicar, 29
Doncaster, 57
Edge Hill, 37
Elvanfoot, 28
Euston, 26, 44-45, 54, 61, 83
Euxton Junction, 32
Garsdale, 89
Glasgow Polmadie, 11
Gleneagles, 59
Golbourne, 49, 66
Grayrigg, 72
Greskine, 62
Hamburg Altona, 134
Hartford, 51, 53
Hellifield, 88
Hest Bank, 25, 34, 62
Ince Central Wagon Works, 76
La Salle, USA, 134
Leeds City, 40
Leyland, 34, 37, 70
Liverpool Lime St, 57
Llandudno Junction, 69-70
Longsight, 57
Madeley, 36
Manchester London Rd, 31-32
Minshull Vernon, 124
Nuneaton, 65
Oceanport, New Jersey, USA, 131
Oubeck, 99, 125
Oxenholme, 60, 68
Penrith, 60
Perth, 79, 101
Preston, 27, 71, 123
Preston Brook, 48
Ribblehead, 87

Roanoke, Virginia, USA, 134
Shap, 28, 33, 47, 104
Shap Quarry, 67-68
Shrewsbury, 136
Skew Bridge, 64, 69
Stafford, 61
Standish Junction, 64
St. Helens, 71
Stirling, 85
Stockport, 52
Swindon Works, 115
Tamworth, 30, 42
Thrimby Grange, 35
Verdins, 46
Warrington, 67
Wigan, 29, 44, 50
Willesden Exhibition, 58
Willington, 125
Winsford, 53
Winwick Junction, 49
Winwick Quay, 31

Location – Colour
Beattock, 142, 149
Birmingham New St, 153
Bourne End, 143
Camden, 140, 150
Carlisle Citadel, 138, 141, 160
Carlisle Kingmoor, 152
Carlisle Upperby, 140, 154, 162
Carnforth, 157
Carstairs, 146
Colwich, 144
Crewe North, 139
Crewe station, 162-163
Crewe Works, 138

Dent, 116
Dillicar, 146-147, 152
Doncaster, 165
Duffield, 117
Edinburgh Princes St, 161
Euston, 137, 139, 145
Greenholme, 153, 156
Harthope, 148
Holyhead, 158
Kirkby Stephen, 109
Lancaster, 105, 143-144, 155
Lamington, 151
Lichfield, 148
Moore Troughs, 151
Nuneaton, 160
Penrith, 107
Perth, 156
Polquhap, 147
Preston, 105
Scout Green, 106, 145, 157
Shap, 107-108, 141-142, 149
Swindon, 161
Tyseley Works, 117-118, 164
Willesden, 159, 163
Winwick Junction, 155
York Museum, 117-118

Locomotives – Black & White
44865, 58
45142, 45
45466, 47
46200, 75
46202, 136
46220, 57
46221, 35, 63
46225, 28, 48, 58, 67, 71, 76
46226, 34, 51, 76
46227, 42
46228, 10-11, 64, 69-70
46229, 29, 31-32, 77, 83, 87-89, 99, 114-116,
46230, 38, 48
46231, 34
46232, 29-30
46233, 104, 123-125
46234, 30, 33, 42, 101
46235, 85, 126-127

46236, 45, 59
46237, 37, 59, 66
46238, 32, 60, 64-65, 68-69, 76
46239, 26, 47, 61, 63
46240, 28, 30, 36, 45, 54, 61, 65
46241, 35, 51
46242, 11, 25-26, 43
46243, 71, 76
46244, 31, 41, 46, 75, 79
46245, 10, 36, 46, 57-58, 67, 72, 96
46246, 44, 49
46247, 40, 49
46248, 62, 70, 95
46249, 47
46250, 33, 50, 60-61, 76
46251, 63, 72
46252, 38, 41, 57
46253, 52-53
46254, 27, 52, 67, 96
46255, 37, 43, 62, 73
46256, 50, 53, 66, 73-74, 135
46257, 27, 44, 75
47667, 51
60010 (4489), 119
60800 (4771), 116
60802, 52
71000, 136
76085, 57
E3076, 59
DB 01.1100, 135
DB 10.001, 135
Deutsche Reichsbahn 05.002, 134
New York Central RR 5424, 132
New York Central RR 5436, 132
New York Central RR 5453, 133
New York Central 6001, 133
New York Central 6024, 133
Norfolk & Western RR 600, 134
Paris-Orleans 3566, 130
Pennsylvania RR 1361, 131
Pennsylvania RR 3768, 132
SNCF 242 A 1, 131
Union Pacific RR 8444, 134

Locomotives – Colour
7022, 161
44770, 158

45082, 151
46220, 139
46221, 138
46223, 147
46225, 140, 143, 155, 157
46226, 141
46227, 142, 148
46228, 148
46229, 116-120, 143, 164-5
46230, 147, 151
46232, 138
46233, 105-109, 163, 165
46237, 154
46238, 145, 152, 154, 156, 158
46239, 144
46240, 138, 140, 159
46241, 144
46242, 152
46244, 146, 149, 156
46245, 137, 140, 149, 153, 162-163
46246, 150
46247, 142
46248, 153
46250, 155, 162
46251, 151, 161
46254, 139, 146
46255, 145
46256, 157, 160
Models, 166-167
Nameplates, 168

Logs
G&SWR route Scotland
46249, Dumfries – Kilmarnock, 15

WCML Carlisle – Crewe
46229, Shap Trial 1995, 89-90
46229, Les Jackson's last run, 1996, 98-99
46233, Down Railtour, Shap trial comparison, 90-91
46233, Down Railtours, 103-104
46235, 3.48pm TTHFO Crewe – Carlisle, 84
46240, Down Royal Scot, 19-20
46242, Up Caledonian, 17
46244, 9.50pm Perth sleeper, 39-40

46245, Up Caledonian, 21-23
46254, Down Lakes Express, 82
Various, Up Caledonian 1958, 18
Various, Down Caledonian,1958, 19

WCML South of Crewe
46244, Watford – Crewe, 12-13
46245, Up Caledonian, 23
46254, Down Lakes Express, 80-82
Various, Down Midday Scot, 15
Various Down Caledonian 1958, 19
Various, Up Caledonian 1958, 18

WCML Scotland
46245, Down Caledonian, 20-21
46245, Up Caledonian, 21-22

Settle & Carlisle
46229, Down Railtour footplate, 86-87

Other routes
46233, Kings Cross – Peterboro', 122

Performance (descriptive)
G&SWR route Scotland
46230 Dumfries – Kilmarnock, 15

WCML North of Crewe
46221, Down Royal Scot, 14
46221, Down Caledonian, 14
46225, Down Midday Scot, 16
46228, Down Midday Scot, 14
46228, Down relief, 1963, 55
46229, Down Lakes Express, 83
46229, Les Jackson's last run, 1996, 96-98
46233, Down Railtour, Shap trial comparison, 90
46233, Up Railtour, 91
46233, Down Railtours, 102, 121-122
46235, 3.48pm TTHFO, Crewe Glasgow, 83
46237, 11.45pm FO Edinboro' – B'ham, 86
46238, 8.55pm FO Glasgow, 80
46238, Down Lakes Express, 83
46241, B'ham – Carlisle, 14

46242, Down Royal Scot, 18
46244, Up Caledonian record run, 16
46244, Down Caledonian, 18
46244, Down Royal Scot, 78
46247, Down Royal Scot, 14
46248, Down Royal Highlander, 93-95
46250, 11.45pm FO Edinboro' – B'ham, 86

WCML South of Crewe
46225, 10.25am and 1.5pm Euston, 78-79
46228, Up Holyhead relief 1964, 56
46228, 4.40pm Liverpool, 78
46229, Down Lakes Express, 82-83
46238, 8.55pm FO Glasgow, 80
46238, Down Lakes Express, 83
46239, 8.5am Euston – Holyhead, 56
46240, Down relief to Holyhead, 1964, 56
46242, Up Caledonian, 18
46244, Up Caledonian record run, 16-17
46244, Down Caledonian, 18
46248, Down Royal Highlander, 93-94
46257, Up Perth – Euston, 100
71000, Down Midday Scot, 14-15

WCML Scotland
46220, Up Glasgow, 92
46232, 8.55pm FO Glasgow, 78
46242, Up Caledonian, 17
46244, 8.55pm FO Glasgow, 79
46244, Up Glasgow snowdrift, 100

Settle & Carlisle
46229, Down Railtour, footplate, 88
46229, Shap Trial return via Ais Gill, 90
46229, Up Cumbrian Mountain Express, 113

Other Routes
46229, Welsh Marches Pullman, 113
46233, Kings Cross –Darlington, 122-123
46233, Darlington – Kings Cross, 123

Text – The Princess Coronation Pacifics
Allocations, 1957, 13
Allocations, 1960, 39
Allocations, Final, 54-55
Allocations 1958-1964, 173-174
Annual mileage, 24-25
Last workings, 55-56
Livery, 123, 171-172
Performance summary, 129-130
Preservation, 112-113, 121
Royal train usage, 55, 57, 121
Slipping problems, 16, 93, 111-112, 130
Statistics, 170-171
Storage, 54-55
Streamlining, 113
Weight diagrams, 169-170
Withdrawal, 54-56
Works maintenance, 110-111

Text – Other Subjects
Andrew, Bill, 6-7, 92, 101, 103-104
Bevils Club, 14
Bibliography, 176
Cadman, Neil, 6-7, 92, 100-101
Caledonian, The, 13
Chapelon, André, 128
Coleman, Tom, 9
Collier, Keith, 6-7, 92, 110-111, 129
Coronation Scot, 9
Crewe North 'Perth Link', 92-93, 100
Diesel Performances, 24
Fowler, Henry, 9
Harrow & Wealdstone accident, 129
Heddon, Gordon, 6, 92
Ivatt, Henry G, 9
Jackson, Les, 6-7, 92-99
Locomotive Exchanges 1948, 9-10
Locomotive liveries, 10-11
Mainline departures from Euston to Crewe, 1960, 174-175
Meanley, Bob, 6
Mechanical stoker proposal, 129
Mile-a-minute schedules, 12
Named Expresses, 14

Perth – Dundee/Aberdeen fill-in turns, 16
Princess Coronation 4-6-4 development, 128
Stanier, Sir William, 9
Theoretical max performance with stoker, 24
Timetable, 1957, 12-13
Timetable, 1960, 39, 174-175
Timetable decelerations, 13, 21
Timetable recovery time, 13, 21
Transfer to Southern Region proposal, 56
Turbomotive, The, 128